CAMBRIDGE TEXTS IN THE
HISTORY OF PHILOSOPHY

IMMANUEL KANT
Groundwork of the Metaphysics of Morals

CAMBRIDGE TEXTS IN THE HISTORY OF PHILOSOPHY

Series editors
KARL AMERIKS
Professor of Philosophy at the University of Notre Dame

DESMOND M. CLARKE
Professor of Philosophy at University College Cork

The main objective of Cambridge Texts in the History of Philosophy is to expand the range, variety and quality of texts in the history of philosophy which are available in English. The series includes texts by familiar names (such as Descartes and Kant) and also by less well-known authors. Wherever possible, texts are published in complete and unabridged form, and translations are specially commissioned for the series. Each volume contains a critical introduction together with a guide to further reading and any necessary glossaries and textual apparatus. The volumes are designed for student use at undergraduate and postgraduate level and will be of interest not only to students of philosophy but also to a wider audience of readers in the history of science, the history of theology and the history of ideas.

For a list of titles published in the series, please see end of book.

IMMANUEL KANT

Groundwork of the Metaphysics of Morals

TRANSLATED AND EDITED BY
MARY GREGOR

WITH AN INTRODUCTION BY
CHRISTINE M. KORSGAARD
Harvard University

CAMBRIDGE
UNIVERSITY PRESS

PUBLISHED BY THE PRESS SYNDICATE OF THE UNIVERSITY OF CAMBRIDGE
The Pitt Building, Trumpington Street, Cambridge CB2 1RP, United Kingdom

CAMBRIDGE UNIVERSITY PRESS
The Edinburgh Building, Cambridge CB2 2RU, United Kingdom
40 West 20th Street, New York, NY 10011–4211, USA
10 Stamford Road, Oakleigh, Melbourne 3166, Australia

First published 1998

Printed in the United Kingdom at the University Press, Cambridge

Typeset in 10/12 Ehrhardt

A catalogue record for this book is available from the British Library

Library of Congress cataloguing in publication data
Kant, Immanuel, 1724–1804.
[Grundlegung zur Metaphysik der Sitten. English]
Groundwork of the metaphysics of morals/ Immanuel Kant;
translated and edited by Mary Gregor; with an introduction by
Christine M. Korsgaard.
p.   cm. – (Cambridge texts in the history of philosophy)
Includes bibliographical references and index.
ISBN 0 521 62235 2 (hardback). – ISBN 0 521 62695 1 (paperback)
1. Ethics – Early works to 1800.   I. Gregor, Mary J.   II. Title.   III. Series.
B2766.E6G7 1998
170–dc21 97–30153 CIP

ISBN 0 521 62235 2 hardback
ISBN 0 521 62695 1 paperback

CP

Contents

Introduction

A life devoted to the pursuit of philosophical discovery may be inwardly as full of drama and event – of obstacle and overcoming, battle and victory, challenge and conquest – as that of any general, politician, or explorer, and yet be outwardly so quiet and routine as to defy biographical narration. Immanuel Kant was born in 1724 in Königsberg, East Prussia, to a Pietist family of modest means.[1] Encouraged by his mother and the family pastor to pursue the career marked out by his intellectual gifts, Kant attended the University of Königsberg, and then worked for a time as a private tutor in the homes of various families in the neighborhood, while pursuing his researches in natural science. Later he got a position as a *Privatdozent*, an unsalaried lecturer who is paid by student fees, at the University. There Kant lectured on logic, metaphysics, ethics, geography, anthropology, mathematics, the foundations of natural science, and physics. In 1770, he finally obtained a regular professorship, the Chair of Logic and Metaphysics, at Königsberg. Because of limited means and variable health, Kant never married or travelled. He remained in the Königsberg area, a quiet, hardworking scholar and teacher, until his death in 1804.

But some time in the 1770s – we do not know exactly when – Kant began to work out ideas that were destined to challenge our conception of reason's relationship – and so of our own relationship – to the world around us. Kant himself compared his system to that of Copernicus, which explained the ordering of the heavens by turning them inside out, that is, by removing the earth – the human world – from the center, and making it revolve around the sun instead. Kant's own revolution also turns the world inside out, but in a very different way, for it places humanity back in the center. For Kant argued that the rational order which the metaphysician looks for in the world is neither something that we discover through experience, nor something that our reason assures us must be there. Instead, it is something which we human beings impose upon the world, in part through the construction of our knowledge, but also, in a different way, through our actions.

The implications for moral philosophy, first presented in the

---

[1] Pietism was a religious movement which emphasized inner religious experience, self-examination, and morally good works. Its emphasis on the importance of morality is often thought to have been a strong influence on Kant.

Groundwork of the Metaphysics of Morals, are profound. The *Groundwork* is an acknowledged philosophical classic, an introduction to one of
the most influential accounts of our moral nature which the tradition
has ever produced. Some of its central themes – that every human being
is an end in himself or herself, not to be used as a mere means by others;
that respect for one's own humanity finds its fullest expression in
respect for that of others; and that morality is freedom, and evil a form
of enslavement – have become not only well-established themes in moral
philosophy, but also part of our moral culture.

But the *Groundwork* owes its popularity to its power, not to its accessi-
bility. For like all of Kant's works, it is a difficult book. It is couched in
the technical vocabulary which Kant developed for the presentation of
his ideas. It presents us with a single, continuous argument, each of
whose steps is itself an argument, which runs the length of the book.
But the particular arguments which make up the whole are sufficiently
difficult in themselves that their contribution to the larger argument is
easy to lose sight of. The main aim of this Introduction will be to provide a kind of road map through the book, by showing how the material
presented in each of the main sections contributes to the argument as a
whole. First, however, we must situate the project of the *Groundwork*
within Kant's general project, and explain some of the basic terminology
he employs.

Kant's philosophical project

Kant was led to his revolutionary views about reason through an investigation of the question "What contribution does pure reason make to our
knowledge of the world and to the government of our actions?" The
empiricists of Kant's day had claimed that all of our knowledge, as well
as our moral ideas, is derived from experience. The more extreme of the
rationalists, on the other hand, believed that, at least in principle, all
truths could be derived from self-evident rational principles. And all
rationalists believe that at least some important truths, such as the existence of God, the immortality of the soul, and truths about what we
ought to do, are either self-evident or can be deductively proved. In
order to formulate the issue between these two schools of thought more
clearly, Kant employed two distinctions that apply to judgments. Since
he uses these two distinctions in the *Groundwork* in order to formulate
the question he wants to raise about morality, it is necessary for the
reader to be acquainted with them.

The first is the analytic/synthetic distinction, which concerns what
makes a judgment true or false. A judgment is analytic if the predicate is
contained in the concept of the subject; otherwise, the predicate adds
something new to our conception of the subject and the judgment is

synthetic. Analytic judgments are, roughly, true by definition: when we say that a moon is a satellite of a planet, we are not reporting the results of an astronomical discovery, but explaining the meaning of a term. The second is the *a priori/a posteriori* distinction, which concerns the way we know a judgment is true. A judgment is known *a posteriori* if it is known from experience, while it is *a priori* if our knowledge of it is independent of any particular experience. Putting these two distinctions together yields three possible types of judgment. If a judgment is analytically true, we know this *a priori*, for we do not need experience to tell us what is contained in our concepts. For this reason, there are no analytic *a posteriori* judgments. If a judgment is known *a posteriori*, or from experience, it must be synthetic, for the subject and the predicate are "synthesized" in our experience: we learn from experience that the sky is blue, rather than yellow, because we see that the sky and blueness are joined. The remaining kind of judgment, synthetic *a priori*, would be one which tells us something new about its subject, and yet which is known independently of experience – on the basis of reasoning alone. If pure reason tells us anything substantial and important, either about the world or about what we ought to do, then what it tells us will take the form of synthetic *a priori* judgments. So for Kant, the question whether pure reason can guide us, either in metaphysical speculation or in action, amounts to the question whether and how we can establish any synthetic *a priori* judgments.[2]

The Preface, and the project of the *Groundwork*

We can make these abstract ideas more concrete by turning to the Preface of the *Groundwork*. Here Kant divides philosophy into three parts: *logic*, which applies to all thought; *physics*, which deals with the way the world is; and *ethics*, which deals with what we ought to do. Kant thinks of each of these as a domain of laws: logic deals with the laws of thought; physics with the laws of nature; and ethics with what Kant calls the laws of freedom, that is, the laws governing the conduct of free beings. Logic is a domain of pure reason, but physics and ethics each have both a pure and an empirical part. For instance, we learn about particular laws of nature, such as the law that viruses are the cause of colds, from experience. But

---

[2] For Kant's own introductory discussion of these distinctions see the Introduction to the *Critique of Pure Reason* (trans. Paul Guyer and Allen Wood, the Cambridge Edition of the Works of Immanuel Kant, Cambridge University Press, 1998). The relevant passages may be found at A 6–11/B 10–14, using the standard method of citing this work, according to the page numbers in the first (A) and second (B) editions. The analytic/synthetic distinction has been challenged in the twentieth century, most famously by W. V. Quine in his "Two Dogmas of Empiricism" (in *From a Logical Point of View*, 2nd edn., Cambridge, MA, Harvard University Press, 1961). How damaging this attack is to Kant's project is a matter of philosophical debate.

how do we learn that the world in general behaves in a lawlike way – that every event has a cause?[3] This judgment is not based on experience, for we can have no experience of every possible event; nor is it an analytic judgment, for it is not part of the concept of an event that it has a cause. If we do know, then, that the world in general behaves in a lawlike way, we must have synthetic *a priori* knowledge. A body of such knowledge is called a "metaphysics." If it is true that every event has a cause, then this truth is part of the metaphysics of nature.

That there must be a metaphysics of morals is even more obvious. For morality is concerned with practical questions – not with the way things *are*, but with the way things *ought to be*. Since experience tells us only about the way things are, it cannot by itself provide answers to our practical questions. Moral judgments must therefore be *a priori*. Yet it is clear that moral laws are not analytic, for if they were, we could settle controversial moral questions simply by analyzing our concepts. So if there are any moral requirements, then there must be a metaphysics of morals, a body of synthetic *a priori* judgments concerning what we ought to do.

The *Groundwork*, however, is not Kant's entire metaphysics of morals, but only its most fundamental part. Kant wrote another book under the title *The Metaphysics of Morals*, in which our duties are categorized and expounded in considerable detail. There the reader may learn what conclusions Kant himself thought could be derived from his theory about a wide variety of issues, ranging from questions of personal morality – such as the legitimacy of suicide, the permissibility of using alcohol and drugs, the proper treatment of animals, and the nature and conduct of friendship and marriage – to larger political questions, such as the proper form of the political state, the legitimacy of revolution, and the permissibility of war.

This book is only a *Groundwork*, and its aim is to establish the most preliminary and fundamental point of the subject: that there is a domain of laws applying to our conduct, that there is such a thing as morality. Its aim is, as Kant himself says, "the search for and establishment of the supreme principle of morality" (AK 4: 392).[4] That supreme principle,

---

[3] The principle that every event has a cause has been challenged by modern physics; modern scientists believe that at the level of the most fundamental particles and events it does not hold. An obvious question is what impact this has on Kant's argument. Must he give up the idea that the causal principle is a synthetic *a priori* truth, or is it enough for his purposes that events at the macro level must still be causally ordered if the world is to be knowable? For our purposes here, the causal principle may still be used as an example of a synthetic *a priori* truth.

[4] The standard German edition of Kant's works is being issued under the auspices of the German Academy (1900–). The standard method of citing passages from Kant's works, except for the *Critique of Pure Reason* (see note 2), refers to the pagination of this edition, and the page numbers are given in the margins of most translations. The citation method used in this Introduction also gives the volume number in which the work is found. The citation says that the passage quoted is on page 392 of volume 4 of the Academy (AK) edition. A complete English translation of Kant's works is also under way, published by Cambridge University Press under the general editorship of Paul Guyer and Allen Wood.

which Kant calls the *categorical imperative*, commands simply that our actions should have the *form* of moral conduct; that is, that they should be derivable from universal principles. When we act, we are to ask whether the reasons for which we propose to act could be made universal, embodied in a principle. Kant believed that this formal requirement yields substantive constraints on our conduct – not every proposed reason for action can be made universal, and so not every action can be squared with the requirement of acting on principle. We have already seen that the principle that tells us that nature in general behaves in a lawlike way must be synthetic *a priori*, if it can be established at all. In the same way, Kant thinks, the principle that tells us that *we ought to* behave in a lawlike way must be synthetic *a priori*, if ethics exists at all. The project of the *Groundwork* is simply to establish that there is a categorical imperative – that we have moral obligations.

Section I

In each section of the *Groundwork*, Kant carries out a specific project, which in turn forms part of the argument of the whole. In the Preface, Kant says that his project in the first section will be "to proceed analytically from common cognition to the determination of its supreme principle" (AK 4: 392). In other words, Kant is going to start from our ordinary ways of thinking about morality and analyze them to discover the principle behind them. It is important to keep in mind that because he is analyzing our ordinary views, Kant is not, in this section, trying to *prove* that human beings have obligations. Instead, he is trying to identify *what* it is that he has to establish in order to prove that. What must we show, in order to show that moral obligation is real?

The "common cognition" from which Kant starts his argument is that morally good actions have a special kind of value. A person who does the right thing for the right reason evinces what Kant calls a good will, and Section I opens with the claim that a good will is the only thing to which we attribute "unconditional worth." The good will is good "through its willing" (AK 4: 394), which means that it is in actions expressive of a good will that we see this special kind of value realized. Kant does not mean that the good will is the only thing we value for its own sake, or as an end. A number of the things which Kant says have only "conditional" value, such as health and happiness, are things obviously valued for their own sake. Instead, he means that the good will is the only thing which has a value which is completely independent of its relation to other things, which it therefore has in all circumstances, and which cannot be undercut by external conditions.

A scientist may be brilliant at his work, and yet use his gifts for evil ends. A political leader may achieve fine ends, but be ruthless in the cost she is willing to impose on others in order to carry out her plans. A wealthy aesthete may lead a gracious and happy life, and yet be utterly regardless of the plight of less fortunate people around him. The evil ends of the scientist, the ruthlessness of the politician, and the thoughtlessness of the aesthete undercut or at least detract from what we value in them and their lives. But suppose that someone performs a morally fine action: say, he hurries to the rescue of an endangered enemy, at considerable risk to himself. Many things may go wrong with his action. Perhaps the rescuer fails in his efforts to save his enemy. Perhaps he himself dies in the attempt. Perhaps the attempt was ill judged; we see that it could not have worked and so was a wasted effort. In spite of all this, we cannot withhold our tribute from this action, and from the rescuer as its author. Nothing can detract from the value of such an action, which is independent of "what it effects or accomplishes" (AK 4: 394).[5]

When we attribute unconditional value to an action, it is because we have a certain conception of the motives from which the person acted. If we found out, for instance, that the rescuer had acted only because he hoped he would get a reward, and had no idea that there was any risk involved, we would feel quite differently. So what gives a morally good action its special value is the motivation behind it, the principle on the basis of which it is chosen or, in Kantian terms, willed. This implies that once we know how actions with unconditional value are willed – once we know what principle a person like the rescuer acts on – we will know what makes them morally good. And when we know what makes actions morally good, we will be able to determine *which* actions are morally good, and so to determine what the moral law tells us to do. This is what Kant means when he says he is going to "explicate the concept of a good will" (AK 4: 397): that he is going to find out what principle the person of good will acts on, in order to determine what the moral law tells us to do.

In order to do this, Kant says, he is going to focus on a particular class of morally good actions, namely those which are done "from duty." Duty is the good will operating under "certain subjective limitations and hindrances, which . . . far from concealing it and making it unrecognizable . . . bring it out by contrast and make it shine forth all the more brightly"

---

[5] At AK 4: 395–7, Kant supports these ideas with an argument to the effect that in a teleologically organized system of nature, the natural purpose of the rational will would be to realize the good will, or moral worth. Kant argues that in a teleological system of nature, we can never say that an organ, faculty, or arrangement exists to serve some natural purpose unless it is the fittest and best adapted organ, faculty, or arrangement for that purpose. The rational will, Kant argues, is not especially well-adapted to produce happiness or any end outside of itself. Its purpose must therefore be to realize its own value. This argument is offered as a supplement, and the main argument does not depend on it. Kant himself did not believe that a teleological conception of nature has the status of knowledge, although he did consider it an importantly useful way of looking at things. The reader is referred to the *Critique of Judgment* (trans. J. H. Bernard, New York, Hafner, 1951) for Kant's views on teleology.

(AK 4: 397). The hindrance Kant has in mind is that the person of whom we say that he acts "from duty" has other motives which, in the absence of duty, would lead him to avoid the action. When such a person does his duty, not otherwise wanting to, we know that the thought of duty alone has been sufficient to produce the action. Looking at this kind of case, where the motive of duty produces an action without any help from other motives, gives us a clearer view of what that motive is.[6]

Kant proceeds to distinguish three kinds of motivation: you may perform an action *from duty*, that is, do it because you think it is the right thing to do; you may perform it from *immediate inclination*, because you want to do it for its own sake, or you enjoy doing actions of that kind; or, finally, you may perform an action because you are "impelled to through another inclination," that is, as a means to some further end (AK 4: 397). In order to discover what is distinctive about good-willed actions and so what their principle is, Kant invites us to think about the contrast between right actions done from duty and right actions motivated in these other ways. To illustrate this contrast, he provides some examples.

The first one involves a merchant who refrains from overcharging gullible customers, because this gives him a good reputation which helps his business. This is an example of the third kind of motivation – doing what is right, but only as a means to some further end – and Kant mentions it only to lay it aside. The difference between doing the right thing from duty and doing it to promote some other end is obvious, for someone who does the right thing from duty does it for its own sake, and not for any ulterior motive. Yet in order that an action should evince a good will, it is not enough that it should be done for its own sake. This is the point of the other three examples, in which Kant contrasts someone who does an action from immediate inclination with someone who does the same action from duty. For instance, Kant says, there are people

> so sympathetically attuned, that without any other motive of vanity or self-interest they find an inner satisfaction in spreading joy around them and can take delight in the satisfaction of others so far as it is their own work. (AK 4: 398)

A person like this helps others when they are in need, and, unlike the prudent merchant, but *like* the dutiful person, does so for its own sake. A sympathetic person has no ulterior purpose in helping; he just enjoys "spreading joy around him." The lesson Kant wants us to draw from

---

[6] According to a common misreading of the text at this point and of the examples that follow, Kant believes that actions can have moral worth only if they are done reluctantly or without the support of inclination. This is not Kant's view. He focuses on cases in which the moral motive operates by itself because he wants to get a clear view of it, not because he thinks that the presence of other possible motives somehow prevents an agent from acting on it.

this is that the difference between the sympathetic person and the person who helps from the motive of duty does not rest in their purposes. They have the same purpose, which is to help others. Yet the sympathetic person's action does not have the moral worth of the action done from duty. According to Kant, reflection on this fact leads us to see that the moral worth of an action does not lie in its purpose, but rather in the "maxim" on which it is done, that is, the principle on which the agent acts (AK 4: 399).

In order to understand these claims it is necessary to understand the psychology behind them: the way that, as Kant sees it, human beings decide to act. According to Kant, our nature presents us with "incentives" which prompt or tempt us to act in certain ways. Among these incentives are the psychological roots of our ordinary desires and inclinations (as sympathy is the root of the desire to help); later, we will learn that moral thoughts – thoughts about what is required of us – also provide us with incentives. These incentives do not operate on us directly as causes of decision and action; instead, they provide considerations which we take into account when we decide what to do. When you decide to act on an incentive, you "make it your maxim" to act in the way suggested by the incentive. For instance, when you decide to do something simply because you want to, you "make it your maxim" to act as desire prompts.

Kant claims that the difference between the naturally sympathetic person and the dutiful person rests in their maxims. The sympathetic person decides to help because helping is something he enjoys. His maxim, therefore, is to do those things he likes doing. The point here is not that his *purpose* is simply to please himself. His purpose is to help, but he adopts that purpose – he makes it his maxim to pursue that end – because he enjoys helping. The reason his action lacks moral worth is not that he *wants* to help only because it *pleases* him. The reason his action lacks moral worth is that he *chooses* to help *only* because he *wants* to: he allows himself to be guided by his desires in the selection of his ends. The person who acts from duty, by contrast, makes it her maxim to help because she conceives helping as something that is required of her. Again we must understand this in the right way. The point is not that her *purpose* is "to do her duty." Her purpose is to help, but she chooses helping as her purpose *because* she thinks that is what she is required to do: she thinks that the needs of others make a claim on her.

Kant thinks that performing an action because you regard the action or its end as one that is required of you is equivalent to being moved by the thought of the maxim of the action as a kind of law. The dutiful person takes the maxim of helping others to *express* or *embody* a requirement, just as a law does. In Kant's terminology, she sees the maxim of helping others as having *the form of a law*.[7] When we think that a certain maxim expresses a requirement, or has the form of a law, that thought itself is an incentive to perform the action. Kant calls this incentive "respect for law."

We now know what gives actions done from duty their special moral worth. They get their moral worth from the fact that the person who does them acts from respect for law. A good person is moved by the thought that his or her maxim has the form of a law. The principle of a good will, therefore, is to do only those actions whose maxims can be conceived as having the form of a law. If there is such a thing as moral obligation – if, as Kant himself says, "duty is not to be everywhere an empty delusion and a chimerical concept" (AK 4: 402) – then we must establish that our wills are governed by this principle: "I ought never to act except in such a way that I could also will that my maxim should become a universal law."

Section II

Although the argument of Section I proceeded from our ordinary ideas about morality, and involved the consideration of examples, it is not therefore an empirical argument. The examples do not serve as a kind of data from which conclusions about moral motivation are inductively drawn. Instead, the argument is based on our rational appraisal of the people in the examples, taking the facts about their motivation as given: if these people act from respect for law, as the examples stipulate, then their actions have moral worth. Whether anyone has ever actually acted from respect for law is a question about which moral philosophy must remain silent. So demonstrating that the categorical imperative governs

---

[7] Both here and later on in the discussion of the Formula of Universal Law, Kant makes it clear that he thinks the lawlike character of a maxim is a matter of its *form* rather than its *matter*. What does this mean? The distinction between form and matter is an inheritance of Aristotelian metaphysics, in which the matter of a thing is the materials or parts of which it is constructed, while the form is the arrangement of those parts that enables the object to serve its characteristic function. For instance if the function of a house is to serve as a shelter, we would say that the matter of the house is the walls and the roof, and the form is the way those parts are arranged so as to keep the weather out and the objects within protected. The parts of a maxim are usually the act which is done and the end for the sake of which it is done. We can show that the lawlike character of the maxim is a matter of the way the parts are arranged, the form, by considering a triple of maxims like this:

  1 I will keep my weapon, because I want it for myself.
  2 I will keep your weapon, because I want it for myself.
  3 I will keep your weapon, because you have gone mad and may hurt someone.

Maxims 1 and 3 are maxims of good actions, while maxim 2 is of a bad action. Yet maxims 1 and 2 have the same purpose, and maxims 2 and 3 involve the same act. So the lawlike character of the maxim rests neither in the purpose, nor in the act, which are the parts or matter of the maxim. Instead it rests in the way those parts are combined – the form of the maxim. In a good maxim, the parts are so combined that the maxim can serve as a law: everyone could act on it.

our wills is not a matter of showing that we actually act on it. Instead, it is a matter of showing that we act on it insofar as we are rational. A comparison will help here. Showing that the principle of non-contradiction governs our beliefs is not a matter of showing that no one ever in fact holds contradictory beliefs, for people surely do. Nor is it a matter of showing that people are sometimes moved, say, to give up cherished beliefs when they realize those beliefs will embroil them in contradiction. Instead, it is a matter of showing that insofar as they are rational, that is what they do. Kant's project in Section II therefore is to "present distinctly the faculty of practical reason, from its general rules of determination to the point where the concept of duty arises from it" (AK 4: 412). In other words, in Section II Kant lays out a theory of practical reason, in which the moral law appears as one of the principles of practical reason.

It is a law of nature, very roughly speaking, that what goes up must come down. Toss this book into the air, and it will obey that law. But it will not, when it reaches its highest point, say to itself "I ought to go back down now, for gravity requires it." As rational beings, however, we do in this way reflect on, and sometimes even announce to ourselves, the principles on which we act. In Kant's words, we act not merely in accordance with laws, but in accordance with our representations or conceptions of laws (AK 4: 412).

Yet we human beings are not perfectly rational, since our desires, fears, and weaknesses may tempt us to act in irrational ways. This opens up the possibility of a gap between the principles upon which we actually act – our maxims or subjective principles – and the objective laws of practical reason. For this reason, we conceive the objective laws of practical reason as imperatives, telling us what we *ought* to do. The theory of practical reason is therefore a theory of imperatives.

Imperatives may be either hypothetical or categorical. A hypothetical imperative tells you that if you will something, you ought also to will something else: for example, if you will to be healthy, then you ought to exercise. That is an imperative of skill, telling you how to achieve some particular end. Kant believes that there are also hypothetical imperatives of prudence, suggesting what we must do given that we all will to be happy. A categorical imperative, by contrast, simply tells us what we ought to do, not on condition that we will something else, but unconditionally.

Kant asks how all these imperatives are "possible" (AK 4: 417), that is, how we can establish that they are legitimate requirements of reason, binding on the rational will. He thinks that in the case of hypothetical imperatives the answer is easy. A hypothetical imperative is based on the principle that whoever wills an end, insofar as he is rational, also wills the means to that end. This principle is analytic, since *willing* an end, as opposed to merely wanting it or wishing for it or thinking it would be nice if it were so, is setting yourself to bring it about, to cause it. And setting yourself to cause something just is setting yourself to use the means to it. Since willing the means is conceptually contained in willing the end, if you will an end and yet fail to will the means to that end, you are guilty of a kind of practical contradiction.

Since a categorical imperative is unconditional, however, there is no condition given, like the prior willing of an end, which we can simply analyze to derive the "ought" statement. The categorical imperative must therefore be *synthetic*, so morality depends on the possibility of establishing a *synthetic a priori* practical principle.

The Formula of Universal Law

Kant does not, however, move immediately to that task; in fact, he will not be in a position to take that up until Section III. Section II is, like Section I, an analysis. Kant is still working towards uncovering *what* we have to prove *in order to* establish that moral requirements really bind our wills. The first step is to analyze the very idea of a categorical imperative in order to see what it "contains." Kant says:

> when I think of a categorical imperative I know at once what it contains. For since the imperative contains, beyond the law, only the necessity that the maxim be in conformity with this law, while the law contains no condition to which it would be limited, nothing is left with which the maxim of action is to conform but the universality of a law as such; and this conformity alone is what the imperative properly represents as necessary. (AK 4: 420–1)

This is the sort of thing that makes even practiced readers of Kant gnash their teeth. A rough translation might go like this: the categorical imperative is a law, to which our maxims must conform. But the reason they must do so cannot be that there is some *further* condition they must meet, or some *other* law to which they must conform. For instance, suppose someone proposed that one must keep one's promises because it is the will of God that one should do so – the law would then "contain the condition" that our maxims should conform to the will of God. This would yield only a conditional requirement to keep one's promises – if you would obey the will of God, then you must keep your promises – whereas the categorical imperative must give us an *unconditional* requirement. Since there can be no such condition, all that remains is that the categorical imperative should tell us that our maxims themselves must be laws – that is, that they must be universal, that being the characteristic of laws.

There is a simpler way to make this point. What could make it true that we must keep our promises because it is the will of God? That would be true only if it were true that we must indeed obey the will of God, that is, if "obey the will of God" were itself a *categorical* imperative. Conditional requirements give rise to a regress; if there are unconditional requirements, we must at some point arrive at principles on which we are required to act, not because we are commanded to do so by some yet higher law, but because they are laws in themselves. The categorical imperative, in the most general sense, tells us to act on *those* principles, principles which are themselves laws. Kant continues:

> There is, therefore, only a single categorical imperative and it is this: *act only in accordance with that maxim through which you can at the same time will that it become a universal law.* (AK 4: 421)

Kant next shows us how this principle serves to identify our duties, by showing us that there are maxims which it rules out – maxims which we could not possibly will to become universal laws. He suggests that the way to test whether you can will your maxim as a universal law is by performing a kind of thought experiment, namely, asking whether you could will your maxim to be a law of nature in a world of which you yourself were going to be a part. He illustrates this with four examples, the clearest of which is the second.

A person in financial difficulties is considering "borrowing" money on the strength of a false promise. He needs money, and knows he will get it only if he says to another person, "I promise you I will pay you back next week." He also knows perfectly well that he will not be able to repay the money by then. His question is whether he can will that the maxim of making a false promise in order to get some money should become a law of nature. Although Kant does not do this, it helps to set out the test in a series of steps.

The first step is to formulate the maxim. In most cases, the person is considering doing a certain action for a certain end, so the basic form of the maxim is "I will do Action-A in order to achieve Purpose-P." Suppose then that your maxim is:

> I will make a false promise in order to get some ready cash.

Next we formulate the corresponding "law of nature." It would be:

> Everyone who needs some ready cash makes a false promise.

At least where duties to others are concerned, Kant's test may be regarded as a formalization of the familiar moral challenge: "What if everybody did that?" In order to answer this question, you are to imagine a world where everybody does indeed do that. We might call this the "World of the Universalized Maxim." At this point it is important to notice that Kant says the categorical imperative tells you to act on a maxim which you can *at the same time* will to be a universal law: he means at the same time as you will the maxim itself. So you are to imagine that you are in the World of the Universalized Maxim, trying to act on your maxim. For instance, you imagine that you are attempting to secure some ready cash by means of a false promise in a world where everyone who needs a little ready cash tries to secure it by means of a false promise. Now, finally, you are to ask whether you could will this state of affairs, in particular, whether any contradiction arises when you try to do so. Kant says, in the example at hand, that it does,

> For, the universality of a law that everyone, when he believes himself to be in need, could promise whatever he pleases with the intention of not keeping it would make the promise and the end one might have in it itself impossible, since no one would believe what was promised him but would laugh at all such expressions as vain pretenses. (AK 4: 422)

Why is this a contradiction? This question has attracted an enormous amount of philosophical attention and many interpretations have been proposed. The views that have been suggested may be divided into three broad categories.

Proponents of a logical contradiction interpretation think Kant means there is a straightforward logical contradiction in the proposed law of nature. One might argue, for instance, that universalization of the maxim of false promising would undercut the very practice of making and accepting promises, thus making promises impossible and the maxim literally inconceivable.[8]

Kant's use of teleological language in some of the examples has suggested to proponents of the teleological contradiction interpretation that the contradiction emerges only when the maxim is conceived as a possible teleological law of nature. False promising violates the "natural purpose" of promising, which is to create trust and cooperation, so that a universal law of false promising could not serve as part of a teleological system of natural laws.

According to proponents of the practical contradiction interpretation, the maxim's efficacy in achieving its purpose would be undercut by its universalization. In willing its universalization, therefore, the agent would be guilty of the same sort of practical contradiction involved in the violation of a hypothetical imperative. In fact, the maxim in the example is derived from a hypothetical imperative – "if you need some ready cash, you ought to make a false promise" – which in turn is derived from a "law of nature" or "causal law" – namely that false promising is a cause of, and so a means to, the possession of ready cash.

---

[8] For the notion of a practice and the logical dependence of actions falling under the practice on the existence of the practice itself, see John Rawls, "Two Concepts of Rules," *Philosophical Review* 64 (January 1955), 3–32.

In the World of the Universalized Maxim, however, this law no longer obtains. So in willing the World of the Universalized Maxim the agent undercuts the causal law behind the hypothetical imperative from which his own maxim is derived, making his method of getting the money ineffective. Language supporting all of these interpretations can be found in Kant's texts, and different interpretations fit different examples better. The problem of finding a single account of the contradiction test that produces the right answers in all cases is one on which Kantians are still at work.

The question is complicated by the fact that Kant himself thinks contradictions may arise in two different ways (AK 4: 421, 424). In some cases, he says, the maxim cannot even be thought as a universal law of nature: the contradiction is in the very conception of the universalized maxim as a law. The example we have been considering is of that kind: there could not *be* a law that everyone who needs money should make false promises, so the maxim fails what is often called "the contradiction in conception test." Maxims which fail this test are in violation of strict or perfect duties, particular actions or omissions we owe to particular people, such as the duty to keep a promise, tell the truth, or respect someone's rights. But there are also maxims which we can conceive as universal laws, but which it would still be contradictory to *will* as laws: these maxims fail what is often called "the contradiction in the will test." They violate wide or imperfect duties, such as the duty to help others when they are in need, or to make worthwhile use of your talents.[9] Here again, there is disagreement about exactly what the contradiction is. Kant suggests that "all sorts of possible purposes" (AK 4: 423) would have to go unfulfilled in a world in which we had neglected our abilities and in which we could not count on the help

---

[9] In the *Groundwork*, Kant lines up the distinction between the contradiction in conception test and the contradiction in the will test with the traditional distinction between perfect and imperfect duties (described above) at AK 4: 421, and with a less familiar distinction between strict or narrow duties and wide duties at AK 4: 424. This parallel might be taken to suggest that these are just two sets of names for the same distinction, or at any rate that they coincide. But in the later *Metaphysics of Morals* Kant describes a category of duties which are characterized as perfect duties and yet which, because they are duties of virtue and all of those are wide, must be wide (AK 6: 421ff.). Kant explains the distinction between narrow and wide obligation in the *Metaphysics of Morals* at AK 6: 390–4. We have a duty of narrow obligation when we are required to perform a particular action, while we have a duty of wide obligation when we are required to adopt a certain general maxim (e.g. to promote the happiness of others) but have leeway as to how to carry the duty out. This explanation leaves the difference between the two distinctions unclear, and Kant never directly addresses the question how the two distinctions are related. If Kant's considered view is that these two distinctions do not coincide, we are left uncertain whether the contradiction in conception test is best understood as a test for perfect duties, or as a test for strict duties. These rather intricate issues about the categorization of duties matter to the reader of the *Groundwork* because one of the duties Kant uses as an example here – the duty not to commit suicide in order to avoid misery – is one of those apparently identified in the later work as a perfect duty of wide obligation. This should perhaps make us cautious about this example.

of others when we are in need. Since rationality commits us to willing the means to our ends, we must will a world in which these most general means – our own abilities and the help of others – would be available to us.

These examples are offered simply as a few illustrations to show how the categorical imperative works to establish the moral status of our actions. Generally, if a maxim passes the categorical imperative test, the action is permissible; if it fails, the action is forbidden, and, in that case, the opposite action or omission is required. The maxims in the examples fail the test, showing, for instance, that making a false promise is forbidden, and that helping others when they are in need is required. For a more complete account of what Kant thinks morality requires of us, however, the reader must look to the *Metaphysics of Morals*.

The thought experiment we have just considered shows us *how* to determine whether a maxim can be willed as a universal law, not *why* we should will only maxims that can be universal laws. Kant is not claiming that it is irrational to perform immoral actions because it actually embroils us in contradictions. The contradictions emerge only when we attempt to universalize our maxims, and the question why we should do that remains to be answered. It is to this question Kant turns next.

The Formula of Humanity

We have now seen what the categorical imperative says. In order to show that we actually have unconditional requirements, and so that ethics is real, we have to show that this principle is one that necessarily governs our wills. This investigation is in part a motivational one. Although Kant denies that we can ever know for sure that someone has been morally motivated, the moral law cannot have authority over our wills unless it is *possible* for us to be motivated by it. But Kant warns us that we cannot appeal to any empirical and contingent sources of motivation when making this argument. As we saw earlier, the sense in which we are trying to show that the moral law governs our wills is not that it actually moves us, either always or sometimes, but that it moves us insofar as we are rational. So the argument must show that the moral law has authority for any rational being, and this means it must appeal only to the principles of pure rational psychology.

As rational beings, as Kant said before, we act in accordance with our representations or conceptions of laws. But what inspires us to formulate a maxim or a law ("what serves the will as the objective ground of its self-determination") is an end (AK 4: 427). Whenever we actually decide to take action, it is always with some end in view: either we regard the action as good in itself, or we are doing it as a means to some further end. If there are unconditional requirements, incumbent on all rational

beings, then there must be ends that are necessarily shared by all rational beings – objective ends. Are there any such ends?

The ends that we set before ourselves in our ordinary actions, Kant
urges, do not have absolute but only relative value: "their mere relation
to a specially constituted faculty of desire on the part of the subject gives
them their worth" (AK 4: 427). The point here is that most objects of
human endeavor get their value *from* the way in which they serve our
needs, desires, and interests. Just as technology is valuable because it
serves our needs, so pure science is valuable because human beings, as
Aristotle says, desire to know; the visual arts and music are valuable
because they arouse the human capacity for the disinterested enjoyment
of sensory experience; literature and philosophy are valuable because
they serve our thirst for self-understanding, and so forth. Although
these other things are not mere means like technology, yet still their
value is not absolute or intrinsic, but relative to *our* nature. Yet, since we
are rational beings, and we do pursue these things, we must think that
they really are important, that there is reason to pursue them, that they
are good. If their value does not rest in themselves, but rather in the fact
that they are important to us, then in pursuing them, we are in effect
taking ourselves to be important. In that sense, Kant says, it is a "subjective principle of human actions" that we treat *ourselves* as ends
(AK 4: 429).

This suggests that the objective end which we need in order to
explain why the moral law has authority for us is "the human being, and
in general every rational being." Accordingly, the categorical imperative
can now be reformulated as a law instructing us to respect the value of
this objective end:

> *So act that you use humanity, whether in your own person or in the person*
> *of any other, always at the same time as an end, never merely as a means.*
> (AK 4: 429)

Using the same examples he did before, Kant proceeds to demonstrate how this principle can serve as a moral guide. Being of absolute
value, human beings should not sacrifice themselves or one another for
merely relatively valuable ends. Since it is insofar as we are rational
beings that we accord ourselves this absolute value, the formula enjoins
us to respect ourselves and each other *as* rational beings. We should
develop our rational capacities, and promote one another's chosen ends.
Respecting someone as a rational being also means respecting her right
to make her own decisions about her own life and actions. This leads to
particularly strong injunctions against coercion and deception, since
these involve attempts to take other people's decisions out of their own
hands, to manipulate their wills for one's own ends. Someone who
makes you a false promise in order to get some money, for instance,

wants you to decide to give him the money. He predicts that you will not decide to give him the money unless he says he will pay it back, and therefore he says he will pay it back, even though he cannot do so. His decision about what to say to you is entirely determined by what he thinks will *work* to get the result he wants. In that sense he treats your reason, your capacity for making decisions, as if it were merely an instrument for his own use. This is a violation of the respect he owes to you and your humanity.

This example brings out something important about Kant's conception of morality. What is wrong with the false promiser is not merely that he does not tell the truth. What is wrong with him is the *reason* that he does not tell the truth – because he thinks it will not get the result he wants – and the attitude towards you which that reason embodies. Even if he told you the truth, if it were *only* because he thought it would get the result he wanted, he would *still* be regarding you as a mere means. Instead, we must tell the truth so that others may exercise their own reason freely – and that means that, in telling them the truth, we are inviting them to reason together with us, to share in our deliberations. When we need the cooperation of others, we must also be prepared to give them a voice in the decision about what is to be done. This leads Kant to a vision of an ideal human community, in which people reason together about what to do. Because this is the community of people who regard themselves and one another as ends in themselves, Kant calls it the kingdom of ends.

Autonomy and the kingdom of ends

To be rational is, *formally* speaking, to act on your representation of a law, whatever that law might be; but we have now seen that the content or *material* of the maxims or laws on which we act is given by the value we necessarily set upon our own humanity or rational nature. Putting these two ideas together leads us to a third idea, which is that as rational beings we make the law, we legislate it. Suppose, for instance, I undertake a program of scientific research. I am curious, and wish to know; in treating my curiosity as a reason to undertake the research, I am in effect taking it to be good that I should know. Furthermore, since we have a duty to pursue one another's ends, my decision to pursue scientific research involves a claim on others: that they should recognize the value of my pursuit of this end, should not hinder it, and perhaps, under certain conditions, should even offer help with it when I am in need. Thus my choice is an act of legislation: I lay it down, for myself and others, that this research is a good, and shall be pursued. We may say that I *confer a value* upon scientific research, when I choose to pursue it. At the same time, the very fact that I make this claim on others serves as a "*limiting condition*" on my own choice (AK 4: 431). If the end that I choose, or the means by which I choose to pursue it, are inconsistent with the value of humanity, then I cannot legislate it, and my choice is null and void: my maxim is not a law. This line of thought leads to what Kant describes as "the *principle* of every human will as *a will giving universal law through all its maxims*" (AK 4: 432).

This principle, Kant tells us, "would be very *well suited* to be the categorical imperative" (AK 4: 432), because it suggests that the reason we are bound to obey the laws of morality is that we legislate these laws ourselves, that they are our own laws. According to Kant there are two ways in which we may be motivated to conform to a law. Sometimes, we conform to a law because of some interest we have that is served by such conformity – for instance, when the law is supported by a sanction. If disobedience to the law will lead to our being fined, socially ostracized, thrown into prison, or dispatched to hell; or if obedience means we will be loved, saved, rewarded, or well-pleasing to God, we may well be motivated to obey it for those reasons. At other times, however, we obey a law because we endorse the law itself, considered as a law: we think that this is indeed how people in general ought to act, and so we act that way ourselves. Kant calls the first sort of motivation heteronomous, because we are bound to the law by something outside of ourselves – God, the state, or nature – that attaches the sanction to the law. The second kind of motivation is autonomous, because we bind *ourselves* to the law. The principle that we give universal law through our maxims suggests that moral motivation is autonomous.

And on reflection it seems that moral motivation must be autonomous. For if we are motivated to obey a law heteronomously, by a sanction, then the imperative we follow in obeying that law is a hypothetical imperative: *if* you would stay out of prison, or go to heaven, or whatever, *then* you must obey this law. And in that case, of course, the requirement is not unconditional after all. If categorical imperatives exist, then, it must also be true that human beings are capable of autonomous motivation. There can be only one reason why we must do what duty demands, and that is that we demand it of ourselves.

Earlier we saw that, according to Kant's Copernican Revolution, the laws of reason are not something we find in the world, but rather something we human beings impose upon the world. We have now come around to the practical expression of that idea. Kant's predecessors, he believes, failed to discover the principle of morality, because they looked outside of the human will for the source of obligation, whereas obligation arises from, and so can only be traced to, the human capacity for self-government. Morality, on Kant's conception, is a kind of metaphysics in practice. We ourselves impose the laws of reason on our actions, and through our actions, on the world, when we act morally.

The principle of autonomy provides us with a third way of formulating the moral law: we should so act that we may think of ourselves as legislating universal laws through our maxims.[10] When we follow this principle we conceive ourselves as legislative citizens in the kingdom of ends. The kingdom of ends may be conceived either as a kind of democratic republic, "a systematic union of rational beings through common laws" which the citizens make themselves; or as a system of all good ends, "a whole both of rational beings as ends in themselves and of the ends of his own that each may set himself" (AK 4: 433). The laws of the kingdom of ends are the laws of freedom, both because it is the mark of free citizens to make their own laws, and because the content of those laws directs us to respect each citizen's free use of his or her own reason. The conception of ourselves as legislative citizens is the source of the dignity we accord to human beings, a dignity which Kant, bringing the argument full circle, now equates with the unconditional value of a good will. We now know what gives the good will its unconditional value: "It is nothing less than the *share* it affords a rational being *in the giving of universal laws*, by which it makes him fit to be a member of a possible kingdom of ends" (AK 4: 435). But we also now know what we need to do in order to complete the argument. Recall that morality is real if the moral law has authority for our wills. The argument of Section II has not yet shown this, but it has prepared the way, for we now know what has to be true of us if the moral law is to have authority for our wills. We must be autonomous beings, capable of being motivated by the conception of ourselves as legislative citizens in the kingdom of ends. If Kant can show that we are autonomous, he will have shown that we are bound by the moral law. This is the project of Section III.

Section III

Up until now, the argument has proceeded "analytically" (AK 4: 392). By analyzing our ordinary conception of moral value, and our conception of rational action, we have arrived at an idea of what the moral law says – it says to act on a maxim one can will as a universal law – and at an idea of the characteristic in virtue of which a person is governed by the moral law – autonomy of the will. To complete the argument, Kant has to show that we and all rational beings really have the kind of autonomous wills for which the moral law is authoritative. This is not an analytic

---

[10] Kant supposes that his three formulations are equivalent, not only in the sense that they direct us to perform the same actions, but in the sense that they are different ways of saying the same thing. All of them embody the view that a rational being must be governed only by his or her own reason. Yet the claim that they are equivalent has been challenged by commentators, some of whom have argued that the Formulas of Humanity and Autonomy or the Kingdom of Ends are stronger formulas, yielding a more well-defined set of duties, than the Formula of Universal Law.

claim, yet if it is to hold for all rational beings it must be an *a priori* one. When a proposition is synthetic *a priori*, Kant now tells us, its two terms must be "bound together by their connection with a third in which they are both to be found"; that is, it must be deduced (AK 4: 447).

Kant opens the third section by making one of the two connections that his argument requires. The will is the causality of a rational being, for our will determines our actions, and it is through our actions that we have effects in the world. If the will's actions – its choices and decisions – were in turn determined by the laws of nature, then it would not be a *free* will. Suppose that all your choices were determined by a psychological law of nature, say, "a person's will is always determined by the strength of his desires." Although you would always do what you most strongly desire, your will would not, according to Kant's definition, be free. A free person is one whose actions are not determined by any external force, not even by his own desires.

This is merely a negative conception of freedom. But Kant thinks it points us towards a more positive conception of freedom. The will is a cause, and the concept of causality includes the idea of acting according to laws: since we identify something as a cause by observing the regularity of its effects, the idea of a cause which functions randomly is a contradiction. To put it another way, the will is practical reason, and we cannot conceive a practical reason that chooses and acts for no reason. Since reasons are derived from principles, the will must have a principle. A free will must therefore have its own law or principle, which it gives to itself. It must be an autonomous will. But the moral law just is the law of an autonomous will. Kant concludes that "a free will and a will under moral laws are one and the same" (AK 4: 447).

Readers are often taken aback by the ease with which Kant draws this conclusion. In the previous section, Kant showed that moral motivation must be autonomous – that moral laws must be laws which we give to ourselves. So any being who is governed by the moral law must be autonomous. But this argument depends on a reciprocal claim that looks at first as if it were stronger – namely, that any autonomous being must be governed by the moral law. Why does Kant think he has shown this? To see why, consider what the categorical imperative, in particular the Formula of Universal Law, says. The Formula of Universal Law tells us to choose a maxim that we can will as a law. The *only* condition that it imposes on our choices is that they have the form of law. *Nothing determines any content for that law; all that it has to be is a law.* As we have just seen, Kant thinks that a will, as a cause, must operate according to a law. If the will is free, then *nothing determines any content for that law; all that it has to be is a law.* What this shows is that the moral law just is the principle of a free will: to have a free will and to operate in accordance with the Formula of Universal Law are, as Kant puts it, "one and the same."

Freedom and morality are therefore analytically connected. A free will is one governed by the moral law, so if we have free wills, we are governed by the moral law. But do we have free wills? Kant points out that insofar as we are rational, we necessarily act "under the idea of freedom" (AK 4: 448). When you act rationally, you take yourself to *choose* your actions, not to be impelled into them, and you think that you could have chosen otherwise. Even if you act on a desire, you do not take the desire to impel you into the action – you think, rather, that you *choose* to satisfy it. Rational choices are therefore undertaken under a kind of presupposition of freedom. And this being so, Kant proposes, we must, when we make such choices, see ourselves as being bound by the laws of freedom. Rationality requires that we act under the idea of freedom, and freedom is government by the moral law, so rationality requires that we regard ourselves as governed by the moral law. Kant's argument seems complete.

But Kant is not satisfied with the argument.[11] He complains that the argument does not explain the interest we take in the ideas of morality. He reminds us of a conclusion already established: if we are morally motivated, we cannot be moved by any interest outside of morality, for if we do our duty for the sake of something else, we are acting on a hypothetical, rather than a categorical, imperative. But now Kant points out that we must nevertheless *take an interest* in moral ideas if we are to act on them. This is clearest when morality demands that we do something contrary to our happiness. Here, on the one hand, is something you badly want to do, something on which your happiness depends; but you find, on reflection, that it would be wrong. If you are to be moved by this reflection to refrain from the action, the thought that you cannot will your maxim as a universal law must motivate you not to perform the action. You must assign a worth to autonomous action, and to yourself as capable of it, in comparison with which your happiness "is to be held as nothing" (AK 4: 450). The argument, Kant complains, has not shown how this is possible. It has shown how we arrive at the *consciousness* of the moral law, but it has not shown how in such a case we can be *motivated* by that consciousness. And unless we can be motivated this way, we are not after all free and autonomous.

Kant does not doubt that we do in fact sometimes take an interest in autonomous action and in ourselves as capable of it. But for all that the

---

[11] At this point, we arrive at the most difficult passages in the book. There is scholarly controversy over the questions why exactly Kant was unsatisfied, and whether he should have been. Interpretation is complicated by the fact that Kant himself continued to work on this part of the argument in later writings, especially in the *Critique of Practical Reason* (AK 5: 30–50), and the version of the argument he presents there seems, at least on the surface, to be different, although there is also controversy about whether it really is so. In any case, for a full understanding of Kant's views on this point, study of the *Critique of Practical Reason* is indispensable.

argument has shown so far, this may be only because of the importance we already assign to morality itself. If we can do no better than this, the argument will be circular: we will have derived moral obligation from a freedom of will which we have attributed to ourselves only because of the importance we in any case grant to morality.

Now at this point, although Kant does not say so, he begins to appeal to ideas he worked out in the *Critique of Pure Reason*, so a brief digression will be useful. In the *Critique of Pure Reason*, Kant distinguishes two different ways of thinking about the world that are available to us. We can think of the world as it is in itself, or as he calls it there the *noumenal* world, or we can think of the world as it appears to us, or as he calls it there the *phenomenal* world. These two conceptions arise from reflection on our cognitive relation to the world. The world is given to us through our senses, it *appears* to us, and to that extent we are passive in the face of it. We must therefore think of the world as generating, or containing something which generates, those appearances – something which is their source, and gives them to us. We can only *know* the world insofar as it is phenomenal, that is, insofar as it is given to sense. But we can *think* of it as noumenal. This way of looking at things is important here for two reasons.

Part of the project of the *Critique of Pure Reason*, as we have already seen, is to provide an argument for the synthetic *a priori* principle that every event has a cause. The argument which Kant presents there has an important consequence for our task here: namely, that the law that every event has a cause can be established, but only for the phenomenal world, that is, only for the world insofar as it is knowable, and not for the world as it is in itself. Now the law that every event has a cause is at odds with the idea of freedom, for freedom is the idea of a first or uncaused causality, a cause that is not determined by any other cause. The upshot of Kant's limitation of the causal principle to the sensible or phenomenal world is this: freedom cannot be an object of knowledge; the knowable world is deterministic. But this does not mean that there is no freedom, for freedom might characterize things as they are in themselves. Indeed, in a sense we must think of things in themselves this way, for we conceive them as the first causes or ultimate sources of the appearances. This means that what Kant is seeking here cannot be evidence or knowledge that we really are free. In his philosophy, that is impossible. Instead he is asking whether we have grounds for regarding ourselves as free.

And – to return now to the *Groundwork* – Kant does think there are such grounds, provided precisely by this distinction between appearances and things in themselves. For this distinction provides a person with "two standpoints from which he can regard himself and cognize laws for the use of his powers and consequently for all of his actions" (AK 4: 452).When we view ourselves as members of the sensible or phenomenal world, we regard everything about ourselves, including inner appearances such as our own thoughts and choices, as parts of the sensible world, and therefore as governed by its causal laws. But insofar as we are rational beings, we also regard ourselves as the *authors* of our own thoughts and choices. That is to say, we regard *ourselves* as the first causes or ultimate *sources* of these inner appearances. Insofar as we do so, we necessarily think of ourselves as members of the noumenal world, or as Kant calls it here the world of understanding. And because we must think of ourselves as members of the world of understanding, we inevitably think of ourselves as free, and so as autonomous. With this independent reason for regarding ourselves as free, the suspicion of a circle is removed.

Kant is now ready to explain how a categorical imperative is possible – what makes it authoritative for the rational will. We must see ourselves as belonging to both the world of sense and the world of understanding. Insofar as we are members of the world of sense, our choices and actions, like everything else, fall under the laws of nature. But insofar as we are members of the world of understanding, we are free and so our wills are governed by the moral law. Now because "*the world of understanding contains the ground of the world of sense and so too of its laws*" (AK 4: 453), we must suppose that in our capacity as members of the world of understanding, we give laws to ourselves as members of the world of sense. And this is what gives us obligations. The conception of ourselves as members of the world of understanding is a conception of ourselves as self-governing, and so as autonomous or moral beings.

Kant ends with some reflections on the nature and limits of practical philosophy. The argument we have just considered requires that we view ourselves in two different ways. As members of the world of understanding, we are free, yet as members of the world of sense, our actions are determined. Furthermore, determinism is an object of knowledge, or at least a feature of the world in so far as it is known, while freedom is only an object of thought or understanding. The two views we take of ourselves may at first seem incompatible, and, if they are, the fact that determinism is a feature of the knowable world may seem to give it priority. But in fact the two standpoints are so far from being incompatible that both are absolutely necessary. For we realize that *something* must furnish us with the appearances from which the sensible world is constructed, that there must be a world of things in themselves which provides us with the appearances. And we know that if we are ourselves agents, who are the sources of some of these appearances (our own actions), then we must be among these things in themselves.

This is why we affirm that our freedom is real; but this does not mean that we can explain how freedom, or, to put the same thing another way, pure practical reason, is possible. To explain something just is to subsume it under causal laws, so freedom by its very nature cannot be explained. Nor, for a parallel reason, can we explain the interest we take in moral ideas, if we must explain an interest in terms of some other interest that it promotes, or some pleasure that it causes. Yet we can now say more about what the object of moral interest is. For if we act as befits members of the world of understanding, we may claim to be citizens of the real kingdom of ends, the community of rational beings who, through their actions, try to impose a rational order on the natural world of sense. What interests us in morality is

> the noble ideal of a universal kingdom of ends in themselves (rational beings) to which we can belong as members only when we carefully conduct ourselves in accordance with maxims of freedom as if they were laws of nature.

Chronology

1788	*Concerning the Use of Teleological Principles in Philosophy*
1790	*Critique of Judgment*, first edition
1791	*On the Failure of All Philosophical Attempts at Theodicy*
1793	*On the Common Saying: That may be Correct in Theory, but it is of no use in Practice*
1793	*Critique of Judgment*, second edition
1793	*Religion within the Limits of Reason Alone*
1794	Kant is censured by King Friedrich Wilhelm II for distorting and debasing Christianity in *Religion within the Limits of Reason Alone*
1794	*The End of All Things*
1795	*Toward Perpetual Peace*
1796	Kant's last lecture
1797	*The Metaphysics of Morals*
1797	*On a Supposed Right to Lie from Philanthropy*
1798	*Anthropology from a Pragmatic Point of View*
1798	*The Conflict of the Faculties.* Part II, *An Old Question Raised Again: Is the Human Race Constantly Progressing?* is one of Kant's important essays on morality.
1800	*Logic*
1803	Kant becomes ill
1804	Immanuel Kant dies on 12 February

Further reading

The Groundwork of the Metaphysics of Morals is, as its title states, only the groundwork of a more complete ethical system, which the reader will find developed in Kant's other ethical works. In the *Groundwork*'s Preface, Kant mentions his plan to issue a Metaphysics of Morals and seems to suggest that a complete Critique of Practical Reason may not be necessary (AK 4: 391). But in the event he did first write the *Critique of Practical Reason* (1788; trans. and ed. Mary Gregor with an Introduction by Andrews Reath, Cambridge, Cambridge University Press, 1997), the first part of which covers much of the same territory as the *Groundwork*, but in a rather different way. The foundational argument, in particular, is presented very differently, and it is a matter of debate whether the argument really is different, and whether that was one of Kant's reasons for deciding to write the book. But the second *Critique* also explores the connections between Kant's ethical ideas and the ideas of the *Critique of Pure Reason*, and raises important questions about the differences between theoretical and practical reason.

The Metaphysics of Morals (1797; trans. and ed. Mary Gregor with an Introduction by Roger Sullivan, Cambridge, Cambridge University Press, 1996) consists of two parts. In the first part, the *Metaphysical First Principles of the Doctrine of Right*, Kant integrates ideas from his moral theory with elements drawn from the natural law and social contract traditions to produce his own theory of law and the political state. In the second part, the *Metaphysical First Principles of the Doctrine of Virtue*, Kant explicates his views on personal morality. Kant also discussed moral issues in his course lectures, some of which have been published. (These are based on students' notes. Some of them are available in *Lectures on Ethics*, trans. Louis Infield, Indianapolis, Hackett, 1963; others in *Lectures on Ethics*, trans. and ed. Peter Heath and J. B. Schneewind, the Cambridge Edition of the Works of Immanuel Kant, Cambridge University Press, 1997.) In the Introduction to the *Metaphysics of Morals* Kant explains why moral theory falls into these two parts, and in both the general introduction and the introduction to the second part he discusses his theory of moral psychology. For a complete understanding of Kant's views on moral psychology, however, one must turn to an unexpected place – the first book of *Religion within the Limits of Reason Alone* (1793; trans. and ed. Allen W. Wood and George diGiovanni in *Religion and Rational Theology*, the Cambridge Edition of the Works of Immanuel Kant, 1996; or trans. Theodore Green and Hoyt H. Hudson, New York: Harper Torchbooks, 1960), where Kant turned his attention to questions about the nature of choice and moral responsibility.

In Kant's view moral philosophy naturally extends to religion and politics for two reasons. First, Kant believed that political and religious ideas that have had a long history or that recur in many different cultures are likely to have a basis in pure practical reason – that is, in morality. In all three *Critiques*, Kant argues that the rational basis for belief in God and immortality rests in morality, rather than in theoretical proofs or in an inference to be drawn from our observation of the design in nature. The most detailed account appears in the second part of the *Critique of Practical Reason*. In *Religion within the Limits of Reason Alone* and in his class lectures on philosophical theology (available in *Religion and Rational Theology*, the Cambridge Edition of the Works of Immanuel Kant), Kant also explores the rational roots of some of the more particular ideas of religion, such as atonement, salvation, grace, miracles, and the need for a church. In a similar way, the *Metaphysical First Principles of the Doctrine of Right* explores the rational roots of concepts used in the Roman and European legal traditions, such as the concept of a right and of the social contract.

The other reason for attention to religion and politics springs from Kant's conviction that the committed moral agent has a deep need to place faith in some vision of how the kingdom of ends may actually be realized. In the three *Critiques* and in *Religion within the Limits of Reason Alone*, Kant explains how this need may legitimately lead us to hope for a moral deity and an afterlife. But Kant also explored the possibility of a more secular faith in the inevitable progress of history towards the realization of the good. This last idea is touched on at the very end of the *Metaphysical First Principles of the Doctrine of Right* (AK 6: 354–5), and spelled out in more detail in some of Kant's essays on history, especially "Idea for a Universal History with a Cosmopolitan Purpose," "Perpetual Peace," and "An Old Question Raised Again: Is the Human Race Constantly Progressing?" (All of these may be found in *Kant: Political Writings*, trans. H. B. Nisbet, ed. Hans Reiss, 2nd edn., Cambridge, Cambridge University Press, 1991.)

The secondary literature on Kant's ethics in general and the *Groundwork* in particular is vast. A disproportionately large part of it has been provoked by Hegel's famous contention that Kant's Formula of Universal Law is "empty" (see *Elements of the Philosophy of Right* [1821], trans. H. B. Nisbet, ed. Allen W. Wood, Cambridge, Cambridge University Press, 1991). One of the best discussions is to be found in the two chapters devoted to Kant in Marcus Singer's *Generalization in*

Ethics (New York, Atheneum, 1961). Another important discussion is found in Onora Nell (O'Neill), *Acting on Principle: An Essay on Kantian Ethics* (New York, Columbia University Press, 1975).

H. J. Paton's *The Categorical Imperative: A Study in Kant's Moral Philosophy* (London, Hutchinson, 1947; later reprinted in Chicago, University of Chicago Press, 1948, and in Philadelphia, University of Pennsylvania Press, 1971) was a standard commentary on the *Groundwork* in the middle years of the twentieth century. Roger Sullivan's *Immanuel Kant's Moral Theory* (Cambridge, Cambridge University Press, 1989) deals with Kant's ethical theory as a whole and contains an extensive and useful bibliography. Interest in Kant's ethics has been lively since the 1970s, and there are a number of recent collections of essays in which interpretation and reconstruction of the Kantian texts serves as the background to philosophical defenses of his theory. See, for instance, Barbara Herman, *The Practice of Moral Judgment* (Cambridge, MA, Harvard University Press, 1993); Thomas Hill, Jr., *Dignity and Practical Reason in Kant's Moral Theory* (Ithaca, Cornell University Press, 1992); Christine M. Korsgaard, *Creating the Kingdom of Ends* (Cambridge, Cambridge University Press, 1996); and Onora O'Neill, *Constructions of Reason* (Cambridge, Cambridge University Press, 1989). The practical implications of Kant's theory, sometimes for moral issues which Kant himself never had occasion to consider, have also received recent attention. Thomas Hill, Jr. considers such issues as affirmative action, our treatment of the environment, and terrorism in *Autonomy and Self-Respect* (Cambridge, Cambridge University Press, 1991) and in *Dignity and Practical Reason*. Onora O'Neill applies Kantian concepts to the problem of famine in *Faces of Hunger* (London, Allen & Unwin, 1986).

The present flourishing state of work on Kant's ethics owes a great deal to the teaching of John Rawls, who lectured regularly on Kant's ethical theory at Harvard, and whose political theory in *A Theory of Justice* (Cambridge, MA, Harvard University Press, 1971) and *Political Liberalism* (New York, Columbia University Press, 1993) is strongly influenced by Kant's moral theory. Rawls himself has published only one essay directly about Kant, "Themes in Kant's Moral Philosophy" (in Eckart Förster [ed.], *Kant's Transcendental Deductions*, Stanford, Stanford University Press, 1989). But quite a few contemporary defenders of Kant studied with Rawls. *Reclaiming the History of Ethics: Essays for John Rawls* (ed. by Andrews Reath, Barbara Herman, and Christine M. Korsgaard, Cambridge, Cambridge University Press, 1997), a collection of essays assembled in Rawls's honor by his former students, includes eight essays primarily devoted to Kant.

Rawls is not the only contemporary philosopher whose work on ethics and politics has been inspired by Kant's, and the reader may wish to explore what other philosophers have done with Kantian ideas in the construction of their own views. Examples include Stephen Darwall, *Impartial Reason* (Ithaca, Cornell University Press, 1983); Alan Donagan, *The Theory of Morality* (Chicago, University of Chicago Press, 1977); Alan Gewirth, *Reason and Morality* (Chicago, University of Chicago Press, 1978); Christine M. Korsgaard, *The Sources of Normativity* (Cambridge, Cambridge University Press, 1996); Thomas Nagel, *The Possibility of Altruism* (Oxford, Clarendon Press, 1970, and Princeton University Press, 1978); and Onora O'Neill, *Towards Justice and Virtue* (Cambridge, Cambridge University Press, 1996). Kant's impact on moral philosophy remains pervasive and profound.

Groundwork of
The metaphysics of morals

Preface

Ancient Greek philosophy was divided into three sciences: **physics, eth-ics,** and **logic**. This division is perfectly suitable to the nature of the subject and there is no need to improve upon it except, perhaps, to add its principle, partly so as to insure its completeness and partly so as to be able to determine correctly the necessary subdivisions.

All rational cognition is either *material* and concerned with some ob-ject, or *formal* and occupied only with the form of the understanding and of reason itself and with the universal rules of thinking in general, without distinction of objects. Formal philosophy is called **logic,** whereas material philosophy, which has to do with determinate objects and the laws to which they are subject, is in turn divided into two. For these laws are either laws of **nature** or laws of **freedom**. The science of the first is called **physics,** that of the other is **ethics;** the former is also called the doctrine of nature, the latter the doctrine of morals.[a]

Logic can have no empirical part, that is, no part in which the universal and necessary laws of thinking would rest on grounds taken from experi-ence; for in that case it would not be logic, that is, a canon for the understanding or for reason, which holds for all thinking and which must be demonstrated. On the other hand natural as well as moral philosophy[b] can each have its empirical part, since the former must determine laws of nature as an object of experience, the latter, laws of the human being's will insofar as it is affected by nature – the first as laws in accordance with which everything happens, the second as laws in accordance with which everything ought to happen, while still taking into account the conditions under which it very often does not happen.

All philosophy insofar as it is based on grounds of experience can be called *empirical;* but insofar as it sets forth its teachings simply from a priori principles it can be called *pure* philosophy. When the latter is merely formal it is called *logic;* but if it is limited to determinate objects of the understanding it is called *metaphysics.*

In this way there arises the idea of a twofold metaphysics, a *metaphysics*

4:388

[a] *Naturlehre . . . Sittenlehre.* According to the *Critique of Judgment,* the doctrinal (*doktrinal*), as distinguished from the critical, part of philosophy is the metaphysics of nature and of morals (5:170).
[b] *Weltweisheit,* a common eighteenth-century word for *Philosophie*

1

of nature and a *metaphysics of morals*. Physics will therefore have its empirical part but it will also have a rational part; so too will ethics, though here the empirical part might be given the special name *practical anthropology*, while the rational part might properly be called *morals*.[c]

All trades, crafts, and arts have gained by the division of labor, namely when one person does not do everything but each limits himself to a certain task that differs markedly from others in the way it is to be handled, so as to be able to perform it most perfectly and with greater facility. Where work is not so differentiated and divided, where everyone is a jack-of-all-trades, there trades remain in the greatest barbarism. Whether pure philosophy in all its parts does not require its own special man might in itself be a subject not unworthy of consideration, and it might be worth asking whether the whole of this learned trade would not be better off if a warning were given to those who, in keeping with the taste of the public, are in the habit of vending the empirical mixed with the rational in all sorts of proportions unknown to themselves, who call themselves "independent thinkers,"[d] and others, who prepare the rational part only, "hair-splitters":[e] the warning not to carry on at the same time two jobs which are very distinct in the way they are to be handled, for each of which a special talent is perhaps required, and the combination of which in one person produces only bunglers. Here, however, I ask only whether the nature of science does not require that the empirical part always be carefully separated from the rational part, and that a metaphysics of nature be put before physics proper (empirical physics) and a metaphysics of morals before practical anthropology, with metaphysics carefully cleansed of everything empirical so that we may know how 4:389 much pure reason can accomplish in both cases and from what sources it draws this a priori teaching of its own[f] – whether the latter job be carried on by all teachers of morals (whose name is legion) or only by some who feel a calling to it.

Since my aim here is directed properly to moral philosophy, I limit the question proposed only to this: is it not thought to be of the utmost necessity to work out for once a pure moral philosophy, completely cleansed of everything that may be only empirical and that belongs to anthropology? For, that there must be such a philosophy is clear of itself from the common idea of duty and of moral laws. Everyone must grant that a law, if it is to hold morally, that is, as a ground of an obligation, must carry with it absolute necessity; that, for example, the command "thou

---

[c] *eigentlich Moral*, perhaps, "morals strictly speaking." *Moral* and *Sitten* are translated as "morals," *Moralität* and *Sittlichkeit* as "morality," *sittliche Weltweisheit* and *Moralphilosophie* as "moral philosophy," and *Sittenlehre* as "the doctrine of morals." Kant occasionally uses *Moral* in the sense of "moral philosophy."

[d] *Selbstdenker*

[e] *Grübler*

[f] *sie selbst diese ihre Belehrung a priori schöpfe*

shalt not lie" does not hold only for human beings, as if other rational beings did not have to heed it, and so with all other moral laws properly so called; that, therefore, the ground of obligation here must not be sought in the nature of the human being or in the circumstances of the world in which he is placed, but a priori simply in concepts of pure reason; and that any other precept, which is based on principles of mere experience – even if it is universal in a certain respect – insofar as it rests in the least part on empirical grounds, perhaps only in terms of a motive,^{g} can indeed be called a practical rule but never a moral law.

Thus, among practical cognitions, not only do moral laws, along with their principles, differ essentially from all the rest,^{h} in which there is something empirical, but all moral philosophy is based entirely on its pure part; and when it is applied to the human being it does not borrow the least thing from acquaintance with him (from anthropology) but gives to him, as a rational being, laws a priori, which no doubt still require a judgment sharpened by experience, partly to distinguish in what cases they are applicable and partly to provide them with access^i to the will of the human being and efficacy for his fulfillment of them;^{j} for the human being is affected by so many inclinations that, though capable of the idea of a practical pure reason, he is not so easily able to make it effective *in concreto* in the conduct of his life.

A metaphysics of morals is therefore indispensably necessary, not merely because of a motive to speculation – for investigating the source of the practical basic principles^k that lie a priori in our reason – but also because morals themselves remain subject to all sorts of corruption as long as we are without that clue^l and supreme norm by which to appraise them correctly. For, in the case of what is to be morally good it is not enough that it *conform* with the moral law but it must also be done *for the sake of the law*; without this, that conformity is only very contingent and precarious, since a ground that is not moral will indeed now and then produce actions in conformity with the law, but it will also often produce actions contrary to the

4:390

---

^{g} *Bewegungsgründe.* Kant subsequently (4:427) distinguishes this from an "incentive" (*Triebfeder*), and the force of some passages depends upon this distinction. However, he does not abide by the distinction, and no attempt has been made to bring his terminology into accord with it. He occasionally uses *Bewegursache,* in which case "motive," which seems to be the most general word available, has been used.

^{h} Here, as elsewhere, the difference between German and English punctuation creates difficulties. It is not altogether clear from the context whether the clause "in which there is something empirical" is restrictive or nonrestrictive.

^{i} Or "entry," "admission," *Eingang*

^{j} *Nachdruck zur Ausübung*

^{k} *Grundsätze.* Kant does not draw a consistent distinction between *Grundsatz* and *Prinzip* and often uses one where the other would seem more appropriate. *Prinzip* is always, and *Grundsatz* often, translated as "principle."

^{l} *Leitfaden*

law. Now the moral law in its purity and genuineness (and in the practical this is what matters most) is to be sought nowhere else than in a pure philosophy; hence this (metaphysics) must come first, and without it there can be no moral philosophy at all. That which mixes these pure principles with empirical ones does not even deserve the name of philosophy (for what distinguishes philosophy from common rational cognition is just that it sets forth in separate sciences what the latter comprehends only mixed together); much less does it deserve the name of a moral philosophy, since by this very mixture it even infringes upon^m the purity of morals themselves and proceeds contrary to its own end.

Let it not be thought, however, that what is here called for already exists in the celebrated Wolff's^1 propaedeutic to his moral philosophy, namely in what he called *universal^n practical philosophy*, and that we do not therefore have to break into an entirely new field. Just because it was to be a universal practical philosophy it took into consideration, not a will of any special kind, such as one that would be completely determined from a priori principles without any empirical motives and that could be called a pure will, but rather volition generally,^{o} with all the actions and conditions that belong to it in this general^p sense; and by this it differs from a metaphysics of morals in the same way that general logic, which sets forth the actions and rules of thinking *in general,* differs from transcendental philosophy, which sets forth the special actions and rules of **pure** thinking, that is, of thinking by which objects are cognized completely a priori. For, the metaphysics of morals has to examine the idea and the principles of a possible *pure* will and not the actions and conditions of human volition 4:391 generally, which for the most part are drawn from psychology. That this universal practical philosophy also discusses (though without any warrant)^q moral laws and duties is no objection to my assertion. For the authors of that science remain true to their idea of it in this too; they do not distinguish motives that, as such, are represented completely a priori by reason alone and are properly moral from empirical motives, which the understanding raises to universal concepts merely by comparing experiences; instead they consider motives only in terms of the greater or smaller amount of them, without paying attention to the difference of their sources (since all of them are regarded as of the same kind); and this is how they form their concept^r of *obligation,* which is anything but moral,

---

^{m} *Abbruch tut.* For Kant's explanation of this term, taken from the context of rights, see *The Metaphysics of Morals* (6:429).
^{n} *allgemeinen*
^{o} *überhaupt*
^{p} *allgemeinen*
^{q} Or "authorization," *Befugnis.* For an explanation of this term in its moral use, see *The Metaphysics of Morals* (6:222).
^{r} *und machen sich dadurch ihren Begriff*

although the way it is constituted is all that can be desired in a philosophy that does not judge at all about the *origin* of all possible practical concepts, whether they occur only a posteriori or a priori as well.

Intending to publish some day a metaphysics of morals,[2] I issue this groundwork in advance. Indeed there is really no other foundation for a metaphysics of morals than the critique of a *pure practical reason,* just as that of metaphysics is the critique of pure speculative reason, already published. But in the first place the former is not of such utmost necessity as the latter, because in moral matters human reason can easily be brought to a high degree of correctness and accomplishment, even in the most common understanding, whereas in its theoretical but pure use it is wholly dialectical; and in the second place I require that the critique of a pure practical reason, if it is to be carried through completely, be able at the same time to present the unity of practical with speculative reason in a common principle, since there can, in the end, be only one and the same reason, which must be distinguished merely in its application. But I could not yet bring it to such completeness here without bringing into it considerations of a wholly different kind and confusing the reader. Because of this I have made use of the title *Groundwork of the Metaphysics of Morals* instead of *Critique of Pure Practical Reason.*

But in the third place, since a metaphysics of morals, despite its intimidating title, is yet capable of a great degree of popularity and suitability for the common understanding, I find it useful to separate from it this preliminary work of laying its foundation, so that in the future I need not add subtleties, which are unavoidable in it, to teachings more easily grasped.

4:392

The present groundwork is, however, nothing more than the search for and establishment of the *supreme principle of morality,* which constitutes by itself a business that in its purpose is complete and to be kept apart from every other moral investigation. No doubt my assertions on this important and central question, discussion of which has till now been far from satisfactory, would receive a great deal of light from the application of the same principle to the whole system, and of confirmation through the adequacy that it would everywhere show; but I had to forgo this advantage, which would be after all more gratifying to me than commonly useful since the facility with which a principle can be used and its apparent adequacy furnish no quite certain proof of its correctness but, instead, awaken a certain bias against rigorously investigating and weighing it in itself and without any regard for what follows from it.

I have adopted in this work the method that is, I believe, most suitable if one wants to proceed analytically from common cognition to the determination of its supreme principle, and in turn synthetically from the examination of this principle and its sources back to the common cognition in which we find it used. Accordingly, the division turns out as follows:

1. *First section:* Transition from common rational to philosophic moral cognition.
2. *Second section:* Transition from popular moral philosophy to metaphysics of morals.
3. *Third section:* Final step from metaphysics of morals to the critique of pure practical reason.

Section I
Transition from common rational to philosophic moral cognition

It is impossible to think of anything at all in the world, or indeed even beyond it, that could be considered good without limitation except a **good will**. Understanding, wit, judgment³ and the like, whatever such *talents* of mind⁵ may be called, or courage, resolution, and perseverance in one's plans, as qualities of *temperament*, are undoubtedly good and desirable for many purposes,ᵗ but they can also be extremely evil and harmful if the will which is to make use of these gifts of nature, and whose distinctive constitutionᵘ is therefore called *character*, is not good. It is the same with *gifts of fortune*. Power, riches, honor, even health and that complete well-being and satisfactionᵛ with one's condition called *happiness*, produce boldness and thereby often arroganceʷ as well unless a good will is present which corrects the influence of these on the mind and, in so doing, also corrects the whole principle of action and brings it into conformity with universal endsˣ – not to mention that an impartial rational spectator can take no delight in seeing the uninterrupted prosperity of a being graced with no feature of a pure and good will, so that a good will seems to constitute the indispensable condition even of worthiness to be happy.

Some qualities are even conduciveʸ to this good will itself and can

---

⁵ *Geistes*. Compare Kant's use of *Geist* in *Anthropology from a Pragmatic Point of View* (7:225) and of *Geisteskräfte* in *The Metaphysics of Morals* (6:445).

ᵗ *in mancher Absicht*, perhaps "in many respects"

ᵘ *Beschaffenheit*, occasionally translated as "character." "Constitution" is also used to translate *Einrichtung* and sometimes *Anlage*, which is used rather loosely in the *Groundwork*.

ᵛ Kant uses a great variety of words for what could be called "pleasure" (*Lust*) in the most general sense. Although he later draws broad distinctions among pleasures in terms of their origins (e.g., between the pleasure of taste and that of sensation, and between both of these and moral pleasure), these distinctions still leave a number of words problematic. Within the *Groundwork* (4:396) he suggests a distinction between *Zufriedenheit* or "satisfaction" in general and reason's own kind of *Zufriedenheit*, which in that context I have translated as "contentment." However, his vocabulary is not consistent, and I have not attempted to make it so.

ʷ *Mut . . . Übermut*

ˣ *allgemein-zweckmäßig mache*

ʸ *beförderlich*. Compare *The Metaphysics of Morals* (6:407–9). *Befördern* is usually translated as "to further" or "to promote."

4:394

make its work much easier; despite this, however, they have no inner unconditional worth but always presuppose a good will, which limits the esteem one otherwise rightly has for them and does not permit their being taken as absolutely good. Moderation in affects and passions, self-control, and calm reflection are not only good for all sorts of purposes but even seem to constitute a part of the *inner* worth of a person; but they lack much that would be required to declare them good without limitation (however unconditionally they were praised by the ancients); for, without the basic principles of a good will they can become extremely evil, and the coolness of a scoundrel makes him not only far more dangerous but also immediately more abominable in our eyes than we would have taken him to be without it.

A good will is not good because of what it effects or accomplishes, because of its fitness to attain some proposed end, but only because of its volition, that is, it is good in itself and, regarded for itself, is to be valued incomparably higher than all that could merely be brought about by it in favor of some inclination and indeed, if you will, of the sum of all inclinations. Even if, by a special disfavor of fortune or by the niggardly provision of a stepmotherly nature, this will should wholly lack the capacity to carry out its purpose – if with its greatest efforts it should yet achieve nothing and only the good will were left (not, of course, as a mere wish but as the summoning of all means insofar as they are in our control) – then, like a jewel, it would still shine by itself, as something that has its full worth in itself. Usefulness or fruitlessness can neither add anything to this worth nor take anything away from it. Its usefulness would be, as it were, only the setting to enable us to handle it more conveniently in ordinary commerce or to attract to it the attention of those who are not yet expert enough, but not to recommend it to experts or to determine its worth.

There is, however, something so strange in this idea of the absolute worth of a mere will, in the estimation of which no allowance is made for any usefulness, that, despite all the agreement even of common understanding with this idea, a suspicion must yet arise that its covert basis is perhaps mere high-flown fantasy and that we may have misunderstood the purpose of nature in assigning reason to our will as its governor. Hence we shall put this idea to the test from this point of view.

4:395

In the natural constitution of an organized being, that is, one constituted purposively for life,^{z} we assume as a principle that there will be found in it no instrument for some end other than what is also most appropriate to that end and best adapted to it. Now in a being that has reason and a will, if the proper end of nature were its *preservation*, its *welfare*, in a word its *happiness*, then nature would have hit upon a very bad

---

^{z} *zweckmäßig zum Leben eingerichteten. Zweck* is translated as "end" except when it occurs as part of *zweckmäßig, Zweckmäßigkeit*, and *zwecklos*.

arrangement in selecting the reason of the creature to carry out this purpose. For all the actions that the creature has to perform for this purpose, and the whole rule of its conduct, would be marked out for it far more accurately by instinct, and that end would have thereby been attained much more surely than it ever can be by reason; and if reason should have been given, over and above, to this favored creature, it must have served it only to contemplate the fortunate constitution of its nature, to admire this, to delight in it, and to be grateful for it to the beneficent cause, but not to submit its faculty of desire[a] to that weak and deceptive guidance and meddle with nature's purpose. In a word, nature would have taken care that reason should not break forth into *practical use* and have the presumption, with its weak insight, to think out for itself a plan for happiness and for the means of attaining it. Nature would have taken upon itself the choice not only of ends but also of means and, with wise foresight, would have entrusted them both simply to instinct.

And, in fact, we find that the more a cultivated reason purposely occupies itself with the enjoyment of life and with happiness, so much the further does one get away from true satisfaction; and from this there arises in many, and indeed in those who have experimented most with this use of reason, if only they are candid enough to admit it, a certain degree of *misology*, that is, hatred of reason; for, after calculating all the advantages they draw – I do not say from the invention of all the arts of common luxury, but even from the sciences (which seem to them to be, at bottom, only a luxury of the understanding) – they find that they have in fact only brought more trouble upon themselves instead of gaining in happiness; and because of this they finally envy rather than despise the more common run of people, who are closer to the guidance of mere natural instinct and do not allow their reason much influence on their behavior. And to this extent we must admit that the judgment of those who greatly moderate, and even reduce below zero, eulogies extolling the advantages that reason is supposed to procure for us with regard to the happiness and satisfaction of life is by no means surly or ungrateful to the goodness of the government of the world; we must admit, instead, that these judgments have as their covert basis the idea of another and far worthier purpose of one's existence, to which therefore, and not to happiness, reason is properly destined,[b] and to which, as supreme condition, the private purpose of the human being must for the most part defer.

Since reason is not sufficiently competent to guide the will surely with

4:396

---

[a] *Begehrungsvermögen.* For Kant's definition of this term see *Critique of Practical Reason* (5:8 n) and *The Metaphysics of Morals* (6:211). *Vermögen* by itself is sometimes translated as "capacity" or "ability."

[b] *bestimmt.* Except when it has this sense of "vocation," *Bestimmung* and its cognates are translated in terms of "determination."

regard to its objects and the satisfaction of all our needs (which it to some extent even multiplies) – an end to which an implanted natural instinct would have led much more certainly; and since reason is nevertheless given to us as a practical faculty, that is, as one that is to influence the *will;* then, where nature has everywhere else gone to work purposively in distributing its capacities,^c the true vocation of reason must be to produce a will that is good, not perhaps *as a means* to other purposes, but *good in itself,* for which reason was absolutely necessary. This will need not, because of this, be the sole and complete good, but it must still be the highest good and the condition of every other, even of all demands for happiness. In this case it is entirely consistent with the wisdom of nature if we perceive that the cultivation of reason, which is requisite to the first and unconditional purpose, limits in many ways – at least in this life – the attainment of the second, namely happiness, which is always conditional; indeed it may reduce it below zero without nature proceeding unpurposively in the matter, because reason, which cognizes its highest practical vocation in the establishment of a good will, in attaining this purpose is capable only of its own kind of satisfaction, namely from fulfilling an end which in turn only reason determines, even if this should be combined with many infringements upon the ends of inclination.

4:397   We have, then, to explicate^d the concept of a will that is to be esteemed in itself and that is good apart from any further purpose, as it already dwells in natural sound understanding and needs not so much to be taught as only to be clarified – this concept that always takes first place in estimating the total worth of our actions and constitutes the condition of all the rest. In order to do so, we shall set before ourselves the concept of **duty,** which contains that of a good will though under certain subjective limitations and hindrances, which, however, far from concealing it and making it unrecognizable, rather bring it out by contrast and make it shine forth all the more brightly.

    I here pass over all actions that are already recognized as contrary to duty, even though they may be useful for this or that purpose; for in their case the question whether they might have been done *from duty* never arises, since they even conflict with it. I also set aside actions that are really in conformity with duty but to which human beings have *no inclination* immediately^e and

---

^c *Anlagen*

^d *entwickeln.* In the context of organisms generally, and more specifically with reference to man's talents and capacities, this is translated as "to develop." However, in the context of analytic and synthetic propositions, see the Jäsche *Logik* (9:111, *Anmerkung* 1), where it is said that in an implicitly identical proposition (as distinguished from a tautology), a predicate that lies *unentwickelt* (*implicite*) in the concept of the subject is made clear by means of *Entwicklung* (*explicatio*).

^e *unmittelbar.* Kant occasionally uses *direkt* as a synonym; no temporal reference is intended.

which they still perform because they are impelled[f] to do so through another inclination. For in this case it is easy to distinguish whether an action in conformity with duty is done *from duty* or from a self-seeking purpose. It is much more difficult to note this distinction when an action conforms with duty and the subject has, besides, an *immediate* inclination to it. For example, it certainly conforms with duty that a shopkeeper not overcharge an inexperienced customer, and where there is a good deal of trade a prudent merchant does not overcharge but keeps a fixed general price for everyone, so that a child can buy from him as well as everyone else. People are thus served *honestly;* but this is not nearly enough for us to believe that the merchant acted in this way from duty and basic principles of honesty; his advantage required it; it cannot be assumed here that he had, besides, an immediate inclination toward his customers, so as from love, as it were, to give no one preference over another in the matter of price. Thus the action was done neither from duty nor from immediate inclination but merely for purposes of self-interest.

On the other hand, to preserve one's life is a duty, and besides everyone has an immediate inclination to do so. But on this account the often anxious care that most people take of it still has no inner worth and their maxim has no moral content. They look after their lives *in conformity with duty* but not *from duty.* On the other hand, if adversity and hopeless grief have quite taken away the taste for life; if an unfortunate man, strong of soul and more indignant about his fate than despondent or dejected, wishes for death and yet preserves his life without loving it, not from inclination or fear but from duty, then his maxim has moral content.   4:398

To be beneficent[g] where one can is a duty, and besides there are many souls so sympathetically attuned that, without any other motive of vanity or self-interest they find an inner satisfaction in spreading joy around them and can take delight in the satisfaction of others so far as it is their own work. But I assert that in such a case an action of this kind, however it may conform with duty and however amiable it may be, has nevertheless no true moral worth but is on the same footing with other inclinations, for example, the inclination to honor, which, if it fortunately lights upon what is in fact in the common interest and in conformity with duty and hence honorable, deserves praise and encouragement but not esteem; for the maxim lacks moral content, namely that of doing such actions not from inclination but *from duty.* Suppose, then, that the mind of this philanthropist were overclouded by his own grief, which extinguished all sympathy with the fate of others, and that while he still had the means to benefit

---

[f] *getrieben. Antrieb* is translated as "impulse."
[g] *Wohltätig sein.* In view of Kant's distinction between *Wohltun* and *Wohlwollen* (6:393, 450 ff.), *Wohltun* and its cognates are translated in terms of "beneficence" and *Wohlwollen* in terms of "benevolence."

others in distress their troubles did not move him because he had enough to do with his own; and suppose that now, when no longer incited to it by any inclination, he nevertheless tears himself out of this deadly insensibility and does the action without any inclination, simply from duty; then the action first has its genuine moral worth. Still further: if nature had put little sympathy in the heart of this or that man; if (in other respects an honest*ʰ* man) he is by temperament cold and indifferent to the sufferings of others, perhaps because he himself is provided with the special gift of patience and endurance toward his own sufferings and presupposes the same in every other or even requires it; if nature had not properly fashioned such a man (who would in truth not be its worst product) for a philanthropist, would he not still find within himself a source from which to give himself a far higher worth than what a mere good-natured temperament might have? By all means! It is just then that the worth of character comes out, which is moral and incomparably the highest, namely that he is beneficent not from inclination but from duty.

4:399

To assure one's own happiness is a duty (at least indirectly); for, want of satisfaction with one's condition, under pressure from many anxieties and amid unsatisfied needs, could easily become a great *temptation to transgression of duty.* But in addition, without looking to duty here, all people have already, of themselves, the strongest and deepest inclination to happiness because it is just in this idea that all inclinations unite in one sum. However, the precept of happiness is often so constituted that it greatly infringes upon some inclinations, and yet one can form no determinate and sure concept of the sum of satisfaction of all inclinations under the name of happiness. Hence it is not to be wondered at that a single inclination, determinate both as to what it promises and as to the time within which it can be satisfied, can often outweigh a fluctuating idea, and that a man – for example, one suffering from gout – can choose to enjoy what he likes and put up with what he can since, according to his calculations, on this occasion at least he has not sacrificed the enjoyment of the present moment to the perhaps groundless expectation of a happiness that is supposed to lie in health. But even in this case, when the general*ⁱ* inclination to happiness did not determine his will; when health, at least for him, did not enter as so necessary into this calculation, there is still left over here, as in all other cases, a law, namely to promote his happiness not from inclination but from duty; and it is then that his conduct first has properly moral worth.

It is undoubtedly in this way, again, that we are to understand the

---

ʰ ehrlicher. I have translated this as "honest" because Kant gives the Latin *honestas* as a parenthetical equivalent of such derivatives of *Ehre* as *Ehrbarkeit*. However, the context often makes it clear that he is not thinking of "honesty" in the narrow sense.
ⁱ allgemeine

passages from scripture in which we are commanded to love our neighbor, even our enemy. For, love as an inclination cannot be commanded, but beneficence from duty – even though no inclination impels us to it and, indeed, natural and unconquerable aversion opposes it – is *practical* and not *pathological*[j] love, which lies in the will and not in the propensity of feeling,[k] in principles of action and not in melting sympathy; and it alone can be commanded.

The second proposition is this: an action from duty has its moral worth *not in the purpose* to be attained by it but in the maxim in accordance with which it is decided upon, and therefore does not depend upon the realization of the object of the action but merely upon the *principle of volition* in accordance with which the action is done without regard for any object of the faculty of desire. That the purposes we may have for our actions, and their effects as ends and incentives of the will, can give actions no unconditional and moral worth is clear from what has gone before. In what, then, can this worth lie, if it is not to be in the will in relation to the hoped for effect of the action? It can lie nowhere else *than in the principle of the will* without regard for the ends that can be brought about by such an action. For, the will stands between its a priori principle, which is formal, and its a posteriori incentive, which is material, as at a crossroads; and since it must still be determined by something, it must be determined by the formal principle of volition as such when an action is done from duty, where every material principle has been withdrawn from it.

4:400

The third proposition, which is a consequence of the two preceding, I would express as follows: *duty is the necessity of an action from respect for law.* For an object as the effect of my proposed action I can indeed have *inclination* but *never respect*, just because it is merely an effect and not an activity of a will. In the same way I cannot have respect for inclination as such, whether it is mine or that of another; I can at most in the first case approve it and in the second sometimes even love it, that is, regard it as favorable to my own advantage. Only what is connected with my will merely as ground and never as effect, what does not serve my inclination but outweighs it or at least excludes it altogether from calculations in making a choice[l] – hence the mere law for itself – can be an object of respect and so a command. Now, an action from duty is to put aside entirely the influence of inclination and with it every object of the will; hence there is left for the will nothing that could determine it except

---

[j] *pathologische*, i.e., dependent upon sensibility

[k] *Empfindung*. In the *Critique of Judgment* (5:206) Kant distinguishes an "objective sensation" (e.g., green) from a "subjective sensation" (e.g., pleasure) and suggests that misunderstanding could be avoided if "feeling" (*Gefühl*) were used for the latter. I have followed his suggestion, while indicating the German word in a note.

[l] *bei der Wahl*

4:401 objectively the *law* and subjectively *pure respect* for this practical law, and so the maxim* of complying with such a law even if it infringes upon all my inclinations.

Thus the moral worth of an action does not lie in the effect expected from it and so too does not lie in any principle of action that needs to borrow its motive from this expected effect. For, all these effects (agreeableness of one's condition, indeed even promotion of others' happiness) could have been also brought about by other causes, so that there would have been no need, for this, of the will of a rational being, in which, however, the highest and unconditional good alone can be found. Hence nothing other than the *representation of the law* in itself, *which can of course occur only in a rational being,* insofar as it and not the hoped-for effect is the determining ground of the will, can constitute the preeminent good we call moral, which is already present in the person himself who acts in accordance with this representation and need not wait upon the effect of his action.†

4:402 But what kind of law can that be, the representation of which must determine the will, even without regard for the effect expected from it, in order for the will to be called good absolutely and without limitation? Since I have deprived the will of every impulse that could arise for it from obeying some law, nothing is left but the conformity of actions as such with universal law,ᵐ which alone is to serve the will as its principle, that is,

---

*A *maxim* is the subjective principle of volition; the objective principle (i.e., that which would also serve subjectively as the practical principle for all rational beings if reason had complete control over the faculty of desire) is the practical *law.*

†It could be objected that I only seek refuge, behind the word *respect,* in an obscure feeling, instead of distinctly resolving the question by means of a concept of reason. But though respect is a feeling, it is not one *received* by means of influence; it is, instead, a feeling *self-wrought* by means of a rational concept and therefore specifically different from all feelings of the first kind, which can be reduced to inclination or fear. What I cognize immediately as a law for me I cognize with respect, which signifies merely consciousness of the *subordination* of my will to a law without the mediation of other influences on my sense. Immediate determination of the will by means of the law and consciousness of this is called *respect,* so that this is regarded as the *effect* of the law on the subject, and not as the *cause* of the law. Respect is properly the representation of a worth that infringes upon my self-love. Hence there is something that is regarded as an object neither of inclination nor of fear, though it has something analogous to both. The *object* of respect is therefore simply the *law,* and indeed the law that we impose upon *ourselves* and yet as necessary in itself. As a law we are subject to it without consulting self-love; as imposed upon us by ourselves it is nevertheless a result of our will; and in the first respect it has an analogy with fear, in the second with inclination. Any respect for a person is properly only respect for the law (of integrity and so forth) of which he gives us an example. Because we also regard enlarging our talents as a duty, we represent a person of talents also as, so to speak, an *example of the law* (to become like him in this by practice), and this is what constitutes our respect. All so-called moral *interest* consists simply in *respect* for the law.

ᵐ *die allgemeine Gesetzmäßigkeit der Handlungen überhaupt*

14

I ought never to act except in such a way that I could also will that my maxim should become a universal law. Here mere conformity to law as such, without having as its basis some law determined for certain actions, is what serves the will as its principle, and must so serve it, if duty is not to be everywhere an empty delusion and a chimerical concept. Common human reason also agrees completely with this in its practical appraisals and always has this principle before its eyes. Let the question be, for example: may I, when hard pressed, make a promise with the intention not to keep it? Here I easily distinguish two significations the question can have: whether it is prudent or whether it is in conformity with duty to make a false promise. The first can undoubtedly often be the case. I see very well that it is not enough to get out of a present difficulty by means of this subterfuge but that I must reflect carefully whether this lie may later give rise to much greater inconvenience for me than that from which I now extricate myself; and since, with all my supposed *cunning,* the results cannot be so easily foreseen but that once confidence in me is lost this could be far more prejudicial to me than all the troubles" I now think to avoid, I must reflect whether the matter might be handled *more prudently* by proceeding on a general maxim and making it a habit to promise nothing except with the intention of keeping it. But it is soon clear to me that such a maxim will still be based only on results feared. To be truthful from duty, however, is something entirely different from being truthful from anxiety about detrimental results, since in the first case the concept of the action in itself already contains a law for me while in the second I must first look about elsewhere to see what effects on me might be combined with it. For, if I deviate from the principle of duty this is quite certainly evil; but if I am unfaithful to my maxim of prudence this can sometimes be very advantageous to me, although it is certainly safer to abide by it. However, to inform myself in the shortest and yet infallible way about the answer to this problem, whether a lying promise is in conformity with duty, I ask myself: would I indeed be content that my maxim (to get myself out of difficulties by a false promise) should hold as a universal law (for myself as well as for others)? and could I indeed say to myself that every one may make a false promise when he finds himself in a difficulty he can get out of in no other way? Then I soon become aware that I could indeed will the lie, but by no means a universal law to lie; for in accordance with such a law there would properly be no promises at all, since it would be futile to avow my will with regard to my future actions to others who would not believe this avowal or, if they rashly did so, would pay me back in like coin; and thus my maxim, as soon as it were made a universal law, would have to destroy itself.

4:403

I do not, therefore, need any penetrating acuteness to see what I have

---

" *alles Übel. Übeln* is translated as "troubles" or "ills." "Evil" is reserved for *Böse.*

to do in order that my volition be morally good. Inexperienced in the course of the world, incapable of being prepared for whatever might come to pass in it, I ask myself only: can you also will that your maxim become a universal law? If not, then it is to be repudiated, and that not because of a disadvantage to you or even to others forthcoming from it but because it cannot fit as a principle into a possible giving of universal law,^o for which lawgiving reason, however, forces^p from me immediate respect. Although I do not yet *see*^q what this respect is based upon (this the philosopher may investigate), I at least understand this much: that it is an estimation of a worth that far outweighs any worth of what is recommended by inclination, and that the necessity of my action from *pure* respect for the practical law is what constitutes duty, to which every other motive must give way because it is the condition of a will good *in itself*, the worth of which surpasses all else.

4:404

Thus, then, we have arrived, within the moral cognition of common human reason, at its principle, which it admittedly does not think so abstractly in a universal form^r but which it actually has always before its eyes and uses as the norm for its appraisals. Here it would be easy to show how common human reason, with this compass in hand, knows very well how to distinguish in every case that comes up what is good and what is evil, what is in conformity with duty or contrary to duty, if, without in the least teaching it anything new, we only, as did Socrates, make it attentive to its own principle; and that there is, accordingly, no need of science and philosophy to know what one has to do in order to be honest and good, and even wise and virtuous. We might even have assumed in advance that cognizance of what it is incumbent upon everyone to do, and so also to know, would be the affair of every human being, even the most common.

---

^o *allgemeine Gesetzgebung.* This phrase, which recurs frequently throughout Kant's works in practical philosophy, presents a number of difficulties. First, it is not always clear whether, within the compound word *Gesetzgebung,* "universal" is intended to modify "law" or "giving." If the context suggests the latter, I have used "universal lawgiving" and indicated the phrase in a footnote. Second, Kant distinguishes between positive law, which is *willkürlich* ("chosen" by the *Gesetzgeber*) and *zufällig* ("contingent"), and natural law, which can be known *a priori.* See *The Metaphysics of Morals* (6:224 and 227). Since "legislation" and "legislator" suggest "making" laws or enacting positive laws, I have reserved these words for the context of "public right," which is distinguished from "private right" by the existence of legislative, executive, and judicial authorities.

^p *abzwingt.* In *The Metaphysics of Morals,* where the concept of *Zwang* comes to the foreground in the context of moral constraint, Kant sometimes gives *Nötigung* as a parenthetical equivalent of *Zwang.* There *Nötigung* is translated as "necessitation," *Zwang* as "constraint," and (*äußere*) *Zwang* as "external constraint" or "coercion." In more general contexts, however, *nötigen* and *zwingen* are sometimes translated as "forced" or "constrained" or "compelled."

^q Or "have insight into," *einsehe.* On the whole Kant seems to use *einsehen* informally. But see below, 4:446, note q.

^r *so in einer allgemeinen Form abgesondert. Absondern* is sometimes translated as "to separate" or "to set aside."

Yet we cannot consider without admiration how great an advantage the practical faculty of appraising[s] has over the theoretical in common human understanding. In the latter, if common reason ventures to depart from laws of experience and perceptions of the senses it falls into sheer incomprehensibilities[t] and self-contradictions, at least into a chaos of uncertainty, obscurity, and instability. But in practical matters, it is just when common understanding excludes all sensible incentives from practical laws that its faculty of appraising first begins to show itself to advantage. It then becomes even subtle, whether in quibbling tricks with its own conscience or with other claims regarding what is to be called right, or in sincerely wanting to determine the worth of actions for its own instruction; and, what is most admirable, in the latter case it can even have as good a hope of hitting the mark as any philosopher can promise himself; indeed, it is almost more sure in this matter, because a philosopher, though he cannot have any other principle than that of common understanding, can easily confuse his judgment by a mass of considerations foreign and irrelevant to the matter and deflect it from the straight course. Would it not therefore be more advisable in moral matters to leave the judgment of common reason as it is and, at most, call in philosophy only to present the system of morals all the more completely and apprehensibly[u] and to present its rules in a form more convenient for use (still more for disputation), but not to lead common human understanding, even in practical matters,[v] away from its fortunate simplicity and to put it, by means of philosophy, on a new path of investigation and instruction?

There is something splendid about innocence; but what is bad about it, in turn, is that it cannot protect itself very well and is easily seduced. 4:405 Because of this, even wisdom – which otherwise consists more in conduct than in knowledge – still needs science, not in order to learn from it but in order to provide access and durability for its precepts. The human being feels within himself a powerful counterweight to all the commands of duty, which reason represents to him as so deserving of the highest respect – the counterweight of his needs and inclinations, the entire satisfaction of which he sums up under the name happiness. Now reason issues its precepts unremittingly,[w] without thereby promising anything to the inclinations, and so, as it were, with disregard and contempt for those claims, which are so impetuous and besides so apparently equitable (and refuse to be neutralized by any command). But from this there arises a *natural dialectic*, that is, a propensity to rationalize against those strict laws

---

[s] *Beurteilungsvermögen*
[t] *Unbegreiflichkeiten*
[u] *faßlicher*
[v] *in praktischer Absicht*
[w] *gebietet die Vernunft . . . unnachlaßlich . . . ihre Vorschriften*

of duty and to cast doubt upon their validity, or at least upon their purity and strictness, and, where possible, to make them better suited to our wishes and inclinations, that is, to corrupt them at their basis and to destroy all their dignity – something that even common practical reason cannot, in the end, call good.

In this way *common human reason* is impelled, not by some need of speculation (which never touches it as long as it is content to be mere sound reason), but on practical grounds themselves, to go out of its sphere and to take a step into the field of *practical philosophy,* in order to obtain there information and distinct instruction regarding the source of its principle and the correct determination of this principle in comparison with maxims based on need and inclination, so that it may escape from its predicament about claims from both sides and not run the risk of being deprived of all genuine moral principles through the ambiguity[x] into which it easily falls. So there develops unnoticed in common practical reason as well, when it cultivates itself, a *dialectic* that constrains it to seek help in philosophy, just as happens in its theoretical use; and the first will, accordingly, find no more rest than the other except in a complete critique of our reason.

[x] *Zweideutigkeit*

Section II
Transition from popular moral philosophy to metaphysics of morals

If we have so far drawn our concept of duty[y] from the common use of our practical reason, it is by no means to be inferred from this that we have treated it as a concept of experience. On the contrary, if we attend to experience of people's conduct we meet frequent and, as we ourselves admit, just complaints that no certain example can be cited of the disposition to act from pure duty; that, though much may be done *in conformity with* what *duty* commands, still it is always doubtful whether it is really done *from duty* and therefore has moral worth. Hence there have at all times been philosophers who have absolutely denied the reality[z] of this disposition in human actions and ascribed everything to more or less refined self-love. They did not, on account of this, call into doubt the correctness of the concept of morality but rather spoke with deep regret of the frailty and impurity of human nature, which is indeed noble enough to take as its precept an idea so worthy of respect but at the same time is too weak to follow it, and uses reason, which should serve it for giving law, only to look after the interests of the inclinations, whether singly or, at most, in their greatest compatibility with one another.

In fact, it is absolutely impossible by means of experience to make out with complete certainty a single case in which the maxim of an action otherwise in conformity with duty rested simply on moral grounds and on the representation of one's duty. It is indeed sometimes the case that with the keenest self-examination we find nothing besides the moral ground of duty that could have been powerful enough to move us to this or that good action and to so great a sacrifice; but from this it cannot be inferred with certainty that no covert impulse of self-love, under the mere pretense of that idea, was not actually the real determining cause of the will; for we like to flatter ourselves by falsely attributing to ourselves a nobler motive, whereas in fact we can never, even by the most strenuous self-examination, get entirely behind our covert incentives, since, when moral worth is at

[y] *unsern bisherigen Begriff der Pflicht*
[z] *Wirklichkeit* and its cognates are translated indifferently in terms of "reality" or "actuality."

issue, what counts is not actions,[a] which one sees, but those inner principles of actions that one does not see.

Moreover, one cannot better serve the wishes of those who ridicule all morality as the mere phantom of a human imagination overstepping itself[b] through self-conceit than by granting them that concepts of duty must be drawn solely from experience (as, from indolence, people like to persuade themselves is the case with all other concepts as well); for then one prepares a sure triumph for them. From love of humankind I am willing to admit that even most of our actions are in conformity with duty; but if we look more closely at the intentions and aspirations in them we everywhere come upon the dear self, which is always turning up; and it is on this that their purpose is based, not on the strict command of duty, which would often require self-denial. One need not be an enemy of virtue but only a cool observer, who does not take the liveliest wish for the good straight-away as its reality, to become doubtful at certain moments (especially with increasing years, when experience has made one's judgment partly more shrewd and partly more acute in observation) whether any true virtue is to be found in the world. And then nothing can protect[c] us against falling away completely from our ideas of duty and can preserve in our soul a well-grounded respect for its law other than the clear conviction that, even if there never have been actions arising from such pure sources, what is at issue here is not whether this or that happened; that, instead, reason by itself and independently of all appearances commands what ought to happen; that, accordingly, actions of which the world has perhaps so far given no example, and whose very practicability[d] might be very much doubted by one who bases everything on experience, are still inflexibly commanded by reason; and that, for example, pure sincerity in friendship can be no less required of everyone even if up to now there may never have been a sincere friend, because this duty – as duty in general – lies, prior to all experience, in the idea of a reason determining the will by means of a priori grounds.

If we add further that, unless we want to deny to the concept of morality any truth and any relation to some possible object, we cannot dispute that its law is so extensive in its import that it must hold not only for human beings but for all *rational beings as such*, not merely under contingent conditions and with exceptions but with *absolute necessity*, then it is clear that no experience could give occasion to infer even the possibil-ity of such apodictic laws. For, by what right could we bring into unlimited respect, as a universal precept for every rational nature, what is perhaps

4:408

---

[a] *es nicht auf die Handlungen ankommt*
[b] *sich selbst übersteigenden*
[c] *bewahren*
[d] *Tunlichkeit*

valid only under the contingent conditions of humanity? And how should laws of the determination of *our* will be taken as laws of the determination of the will of rational beings as such, and for ours only as rational beings, if they were merely empirical and did not have their origin completely a priori in pure but practical reason?

Nor could one give worse advice to morality than by wanting to derive it from examples. For, every example of it represented to me must itself first be appraised in accordance with principles of morality, as to whether it is also worthy to serve as an original example, that is, as a model; it can by no means authoritatively provide the concept of morality. Even the Holy One of the Gospel must first be compared with our ideal of moral perfection before he is cognized as such; even he says of himself: why do you call me (whom you see) good? none is good (the archetype of the good) but God only (whom you do not see).[e] But whence have we the concept of God as the highest good? Solely from the *idea* of moral perfec-   4:409 tion that reason frames a priori and connects inseparably with the concept of a free will. Imitation has no place at all in matters of morality, and examples serve only for encouragement, that is, they put beyond doubt the practicability of what the law commands and make intuitive[f] what the practical rule expresses more generally, but they can never justify setting aside their true original, which lies in reason, and guiding oneself by examples.

If there is, then, no genuine supreme basic principle of morality that does not have to rest only on pure reason independently of all experience, I believe it unnecessary even to ask whether it is a good thing to set forth in their generality[g] (*in abstracto*) these concepts as they, along with the principles belonging to them, are fixed a priori, if this cognition is to be distinguished from the common and called philosophic. But in our day it may well be necessary to ask this. For if votes were collected as to which is to be preferred – pure rational cognition separated from anything empirical, hence metaphysics of morals, or popular practical philosophy – one can guess at once on which side the preponderance would fall.

This descending to popular concepts is certainly very commendable, provided the ascent to the principles of pure reason has first taken place and has been carried through to complete satisfaction. That would mean that the doctrine of morals is first *grounded* on metaphysics and afterwards, when it has been firmly established, is provided with *access* by means of popularity. But it is quite absurd to want to comply with popularity in the first investigation, on which all correctness of basic principles depends. Not only can this procedure never lay claim to the very rare merit of a true *philosophic popular-*

---

[e] Matthew 19:17
[f] *machen . . . anschaulich*
[g] *im Allgemeinen*

ity, since there is no art in being commonly understandable if one thereby renounces any well-grounded insight; it also produces a disgusting hodge-podge of patchwork observations and half-rationalized principles, in which shallow pates revel because it is something useful for everyday chitchat, but the insightful, feeling confused and dissatisfied without being able to help themselves, avert their eyes – although philosophers, who see quite well through the deception, get little hearing when they call [moralists] away for a time from this alleged popularity, so that they may be rightly popular only after having acquired determinate insight.

4:410

One need only look at attempts at morality in that popular taste. One will find now the special determination*[h]* of human nature (but occasionally the idea of a rational nature as such along with it), now perfection, now happiness, here moral feeling, there fear of God, a bit of this and also a bit of that in a marvellous mixture, without its occurring to them to ask whether the principles of morality are to be sought at all in acquaintance with human nature (which we can get only from experience) and, if this is not the case – if these principles are to be found altogether a priori, free from anything empirical, solely in pure rational concepts and nowhere else even to the slightest extent – instead to adopt the plan*[i]* of quite separating this investigation as pure practical philosophy or (if one may use a name so decried) as metaphysics of morals,* of bringing it all by itself to its full completeness, and of putting off the public, which de-mands popularity, pending the outcome of this undertaking.

But such a completely isolated metaphysics of morals, mixed with no anthropology, theology, physics, or hyperphysics and still less with occult qualities (which could be called hypophysical), is not only an indispens-able substratum of all theoretical and surely determined cognition of duties; it is also a desideratum of utmost importance to the actual fulfill-ment of their precepts. For, the pure thought of duty and in general of the moral law, mixed with no foreign addition of empirical inducements, has by way of reason alone (which with this first becomes aware that it can of itself also be practical) an influence on the human heart so much more

4:411

powerful than all other incentives,† which may be summoned from the

---

One can, if one wants to, distinguish pure philosophy of morals (metaphysics) from applied (namely to human nature) (just as pure mathematics is distinguished from applied, and pure logic from applied). By using this name one is also reminded at once that moral principles are not based on what is peculiar to human nature but must be fixed[j]* a priori by themselves, while from such principles it must be possible to derive practical rules for every rational nature, and accordingly for human nature as well.

†I have a letter from the late excellent Sulzer[4] in which he asks me what the cause might be that the teachings of virtue, however much they contain that is convincing to reason, accom-

[h] *Bestimmung*
[i] *den Anschlag zu fassen*
[j] *bestehend sein müssen*

empirical field, that reason, in the consciousness of its dignity, despises the latter and can gradually become their master; on the other hand a mixed doctrine of morals, put together from incentives of feeling and inclination and also of rational concepts, must make the mind waver between motives that cannot be brought under any principle, that can lead only contingently to what is good and can very often also lead to what is evil.

From what has been said it is clear that all moral concepts have their seat and origin completely a priori in reason, and indeed in the most common reason just as in reason that is speculative in the highest degree; that they cannot be abstracted from any empirical and therefore merely contingent cognitions; that just in this purity of their origin lies their dignity, so that they can serve us as supreme practical principles; that in adding anything empirical to them one subtracts just that much from their genuine influence and from the unlimited worth of actions; that it is not only a requirement of the greatest necessity for theoretical purposes, when it is a matter merely of speculation, but also of the greatest practical importance to draw its concepts and laws from pure reason, to set them forth pure and unmixed, and indeed to determine the extent of this entire practical or pure rational cognition, that is, to determine the entire faculty of pure practical reason; and in so doing, it is of the greatest practical importance not to make its principles dependent upon the special nature of human reason – as speculative philosophy permits and even at times finds necessary – but instead, just because moral laws are to hold for every rational being as such, to derive them from the universal concept of a rational being as such, and in this way to set forth completely the whole of morals, which needs anthropology for its *application* to human beings, at first independently of this as pure philosophy, that is, as metaphysics (as can well be done in this kind of quite separated cognitions);[l] [for we are] well aware that, unless we are in possession of this, it would be – I will not say futile to determine precisely for speculative appraisal the moral element of duty in all that conforms with duty, but – impossible to base

4:412

---

plish so little. By trying to prepare a complete answer I delayed too long. However, my answer is simply that the teachers themselves have not brought their concepts to purity, but, since they want to do too well by hunting everywhere for motives to moral goodness, in trying to make their medicine really strong they spoil it. For the most ordinary observation shows that if we represent, on the one hand, an action of integrity[k] done with steadfast soul, apart from every view to advantage of any kind in this world or another and even under the greatest temptations of need or allurement, it leaves far behind and eclipses any similar act that was affected in the least by an extraneous incentive; it elevates the soul and awakens a wish to be able to act in like manner oneself. Even children of moderate age feel this impression, and one should never represent duties to them in any other way.

[k] *Rechtschaffenheit*

[l] The structure of this sentence, from the semicolon to "impossible to base morals," has been slightly modified.

morals on their genuine principles even for common and practical use, especially that of moral instruction, and thereby to bring about pure moral dispositions and engraft them onto people's minds for the highest good in the world.[m]

However, in order to advance by natural steps in this study – not merely from common moral appraisal (which is here very worthy of respect) to philosophic, as has already been done, but – from a popular philosophy, which goes no further than it can by groping with the help of examples, to metaphysics (which no longer lets itself be held back by anything empirical and, since it must measure out the whole sum of rational cognition of this kind, goes if need be all the way to ideas, where examples themselves fail us), we must follow and present distinctly the practical faculty of reason, from its general rules of determination to the point where the concept of duty arises from it.

Everything in nature works in accordance with laws. Only a rational being has the capacity to act *in accordance with the representation* of laws, that is, in accordance with principles, or has a *will*. Since *reason* is required for the derivation of actions from laws, the will is nothing other than practical reason. If reason infallibly determines the will, the actions of such a being that are cognized as objectively necessary are also subjectively necessary, that is, the will is a capacity to choose *only that* which reason independently of inclination cognizes as practically necessary, that is, as good. However, if reason solely by itself does not adequately determine the will; if the will is exposed[n] also to subjective conditions (certain incentives) that are not always in accord with the objective ones; in a word, if the will is not *in itself* completely in conformity with reason (as is actually the case with human beings), then actions that are cognized as objectively necessary are subjectively contingent, and the determination of such a will in conformity with objective laws is *necessitation:* that is to say, the relation of objective laws to a will that is not thoroughly good is represented as the determination of the will of a rational being through grounds of reason, indeed, but grounds to which this will is not by its nature necessarily obedient.

The representation of an objective principle, insofar as it is necessitating for a will, is called a command (of reason), and the formula of the command is called an **imperative**.

All imperatives are expressed by an *ought* and indicate by this the relation of an objective law of reason to a will that by its subjective constitution is not necessarily determined by it (a necessitation). They say that to do or to omit something would be good, but they say it to a will that does not always do something just because it is represented to it that it

4:413

m zum höchsten Weltbesten
n unterworfen

24

would be good to do that thing. Practical good, however, is that which determines the will by means of representations of reason, hence not by subjective causes but objectively, that is, from grounds that are valid for every rational being as such. It is distinguished from the *agreeable,* as that which influences the will only by means of feeling° from merely subjective causes, which hold only for the senses of this or that one, and not as a principle of reason, which holds for everyone.*

A perfectly good will would, therefore, equally stand under objective laws (of the good), but it could not on this account be represented as *necessitated* to actions in conformity with law since of itself, by its subjective constitution, it can be determined only through the representation of the good. Hence no imperatives hold for the *divine* will and in general for a *holy* will: the "ought" is out of place here, because volition*ᵖ* is of itself necessarily in accord with the law. Therefore imperatives are only formulae expressing the relation of objective laws of volition in general to the subjective imperfection of the will of this or that rational being, for example, of the human will.

4:414

Now, all imperatives command either *hypothetically* or *categorically.* The former represent the practical necessity of a possible action as a means to achieving something else that one wills (or that it is at least possible for one to will). The categorical imperative would be that which represented an action as objectively necessary of itself, without reference to another end.

Since every practical law represents a possible action as good and thus as necessary for a subject practically determinable by reason, all imperatives are formulae for the determination of action that is necessary in accordance with the principle of a will which is good in some way. Now, if the action would be good merely as a means *to something else* the imperative is *hypothetical;* if the action is represented as *in itself* good, hence as necessary in a will in itself conforming to reason, as its principle, *then it is categorical.*

---

*The dependence of the faculty of desire upon feelings is called inclination, and this accordingly always indicates a *need.* The dependence of a contingently determinable will on principles of reason, however, is called an *interest.* This, accordingly, is present only in the case of a dependent will, which is not of itself always in conformity with reason; in the case of the divine will we cannot think of any interest. But even the human will can *take an interest* in something without therefore *acting from interest.* The first signifies *practical* interest in the action, the second, *pathological* interest in the object of the action. The former indicates only dependence of the will upon principles of reason *in themselves;* the second, dependence upon principles of reason for the sake of inclination, namely where reason supplies only the practical rule as to how to remedy the need of inclination. In the first case the action interests me; in the second, the object of the action (insofar as it is agreeable to me). We have seen in the first section that in the case of an action from duty we must look not to interest in the object but merely to that in the action itself and its principle in reason (the law).

° *Empfindung*
ᵖ *das Sollen . . . das Wollen*

25

The imperative thus says which action possible by me would be good, and represents a practical rule in relation to a will that does not straightaway do an action just because it is good, partly because the subject does not always know that it is good, partly because, even if he knows this, his maxims could still be opposed to the objective principles of a practical reason.

4:415   Hence the hypothetical imperative says only that the action is good for some *possible* or *actual* purpose. In the first case it is a **problematically** practical principle, in the second an **assertorically** practical principle. The categorical imperative, which declares the action to be of itself objectively necessary without reference to some purpose, that is, even apart from any other end, holds as an **apodictically** practical principle.

One can think of what is possible only through the powers of some rational being as also a possible purpose of some will; accordingly, principles of action, insofar as this is represented as necessary for attaining some possible purpose to be brought about by it, are in fact innumerable. All sciences have some practical part, consisting of problems [which suppose] that some end is possible for us and of imperatives as to how it can be attained. These can therefore be called, in general, imperatives of **skill**. Whether the end is rational and good is not at all the question here, but only what one must do in order to attain it. The precepts for a physician to make his man healthy in a well-grounded way, and for a poisoner to be sure of killing his, are of equal worth insofar as each serves perfectly to bring about his purpose. Since in early youth it is not known what ends might occur to us in the course of life, parents seek above all to have their children learn *a great many things* and to provide for *skill* in the use of means to all sorts of *discretionary* ends,[q] about none of which can they determine whether it might in the future actually become their pupil's purpose, though it is always *possible* that he might at some time have it; and this concern is so great that they commonly neglect to form and correct their children's judgment about the worth of the things that they might make their ends.

There is, however, *one* end that can be presupposed as actual in the case of all rational beings (insofar as imperatives apply to them, namely as dependent beings), and therefore one purpose that they not merely *could* have but that we can safely presuppose they all actually *do have* by a natural necessity, and that purpose is *happiness*. The hypothetical imperative that represents the practical necessity of an action as a means to the promotion of happiness is **assertoric**. It may be set forth not merely as necessary to some uncertain, merely possible purpose but to a purpose that can be presupposed surely and a priori in the case of every human 4:416   being, because it belongs to his essence. Now, skill in the choice of means

---

[q] *beliebigen Zwecken*

26

to one's own greatest well-being can be called *prudence** in the narrowest sense. Hence the imperative that refers to the choice of means to one's own happiness, that is, the precept of prudence, is still always *hypothetical*; the action is not commanded absolutely but only as a means to another purpose.

Finally there is one imperative that, without being based upon and having as its condition' any other purpose to be attained by certain conduct, commands this conduct immediately. This imperative is **categorical**. It has to do not with the matter of the action and what is to result from it, but with the form and the principle from which the action itself follows; and the essentially good in the action' consists in the disposition, let the result be what it may. This imperative may be called the imperative **of morality**.

Volition in accordance with these three kinds of principles is also clearly distinguished by *dissimilarity'* in the necessitation of the will. In order to make this dissimilarity evident, I think they would be most suitably named in their order by being said to be either *rules* of skill, or *counsels* of prudence, or *commands* (*laws*) of morality. For, only law brings with it the concept of an *unconditional* and objective and hence universally valid *necessity*, and commands are laws that must be obeyed, that is, must be followed even against inclination. *Giving counsel* does involve necessity, which, however, can hold only under a subjective and contingent condition, whether this or that man counts this or that in his happiness; the categorical imperative, on the contrary, is limited by no condition and, as absolutely although practically necessary, can be called quite strictly a command. The first imperative could also be called *technical* (belonging to art), the second pragmatic† (belonging to welfare), the third moral (belonging to free conduct as such, that is, to morals).

4:417

Now the question arises: how are all these imperatives possible? This question does not inquire how the performance of the action that the

---

*The word "prudence" is taken in two senses: in the one it may bear the name of "knowledge of the world,"⁵ in the other that of "private prudence." The first is a human being's skill in influencing others so as to use them for his own purposes. The second is the insight to unite all these purposes to his own enduring advantage. The latter is properly that to which the worth even of the former is reduced, and if someone is prudent in the first sense but not in the second, we might better say of him that he is clever and cunning but, on the whole, nevertheless imprudent.

†It seems to me that the proper meaning of the word *pragmatic* can be most accurately determined in this way. For *sanctions* are called "pragmatic" that do not flow strictly from the right of *states* as necessary laws but from *provision* for the general welfare. A *history* is composed pragmatically when it makes us *prudent*, that is, instructs the world how it can look after its advantage better than, or at least as well as, the world of earlier times.

' *als Bedingung zum Grunde zu legen*
⁵ *das Wesentlich-Gute derselben*
' *Ungleichheit*

27

imperative commands can be thought, but only how the necessitation of the will, which the imperative expresses in the problem, can be thought. How an imperative of skill is possible requires no special discussion. Whoever wills the end also wills (insofar as reason has decisive influence on his actions) the indispensably necessary means to it that are within his power. This proposition is, as regards the volition, analytic; for in the volition of an object as my effect, my causality as acting cause, that is, the use of means, is already thought, and the imperative extracts the concept of actions necessary to this end merely from the concept of a volition of this end (synthetic propositions no doubt belong to determining the means themselves to a purpose intended, but they do not have to do with the ground for actualizing" the act of will but for actualizing the object). That in order to divide a line into two equal parts on a sure principle I must make two intersecting arcs from its ends, mathematics admittedly teaches only by synthetic propositions; but when I know that only by such an action can the proposed effect take place, then it is an analytic proposition that if I fully^v will the effect I also will the action requisite to it; for, it is one and the same thing to represent something as an effect possible by me in a certain way and to represent myself as acting in this way with respect to it.

If only it were as easy to give a determinate concept of happiness, imperatives of prudence would agree entirely with those of skill and would be just as^w analytic. For it could be said, here just as there: who wills the end also wills (necessarily in conformity with reason) the sole means to it that are within his control. But it is a misfortune that the concept of happiness is such an indeterminate concept that, although every human being wishes to attain this, he can still never say determinately and consistently with himself what he really wishes and wills. The cause of this is that all the elements that belong to the concept of happiness are without exception empirical, that is, they must be borrowed from experience, and that nevertheless for the idea of happiness there is required an absolute whole, a maximum of well-being in my present condition and in every future condition. Now, it is impossible for the most insightful and at the same time most powerful but still finite being to frame for himself a determinate concept of what he really wills here. If he wills riches, how much anxiety, envy and intrigue might he not bring upon himself in this way! If he wills a great deal of cognition and insight, that might become only an eye all the more acute to show him, as all the more dreadful, ills that are now concealed from him and that cannot be avoided, or to burden

4:418

" *wirklich zu machen*
^{v} *vollständig*
^{w} *eben sowohl*

his desires,[x] which already give him enough to do, with still more needs. If he wills a long life, who will guarantee him that it would not be a long misery? If he at least wills health, how often has not bodily discomfort kept someone from excesses into which unlimited health would have let him fall, and so forth. In short, he is not capable of any principle by which to determine with complete certainty what would make him truly happy, because for this omniscience would be required. One cannot therefore act on determinate principles for the sake of being happy, but only on empirical counsels, for example, of a regimen,[y] frugality, courtesy, reserve and so forth, which experience teaches are most conducive to well-being on the average. From this it follows that imperatives of prudence cannot, to speak precisely, command at all, that is, present actions objectively as practically *necessary;* that they are to be taken as counsels (*consilia*) rather than as commands (*praecepta*) of reason; that the problem of determining surely and universally which action would promote the happiness of a rational being is completely insoluble, so that there can be no imperative with respect to it that would, in the strict sense, command him to do what would make him happy; for happiness is not an ideal of reason but of imagination, resting merely upon empirical grounds, which it is futile to expect should determine an action by which the totality of a series of results in fact infinite would be attained. This imperative of prudence would, nevertheless, be an analytic practical proposition if it is supposed that the means to happiness can be assigned with certainty; for it is distinguished from the imperative of skill only in this: that in the case of the latter the end is merely possible, whereas in the former it is given; but since both merely command the means to what it is presupposed one wills as an end, the imperative that commands volition of the means for him who wills the end is in both cases analytic. Hence there is also no difficulty with respect to the possibility of such an imperative. 4:419

On the other hand, the question of how the imperative of *morality* is possible is undoubtedly the only one needing a solution, since it is in no way hypothetical and the objectively represented necessity can therefore not be based on any presupposition, as in the case of hypothetical imperatives. Only we must never leave out of account, here, that it cannot be made out *by means of any example,* and so empirically, whether there is any such imperative at all, but it is rather to be feared that all imperatives which seem to be categorical may yet in some hidden way be hypothetical. For example, when it is said "you ought not to promise anything deceitfully," and one assumes that the necessity of this omission is not giving

---

[x] *Begierden.* According to *The Metaphysics of Morals* (6:212), *Begierde* must always be preceded by a feeling of pleasure.
[y] *Diät*

counsel for avoiding some other ill – in which case what is said would be "you ought not to make a lying promise lest if it comes to light you destroy your credit" – but that an action of this kind must be regarded as in itself evil and that the imperative of prohibition is therefore categorical: one still cannot show with certainty in any example that the will is here determined merely through the law, without another incentive, although it seems to be so; for it is always possible that covert fear of disgrace, perhaps also obscure apprehension of other dangers, may have had an influence on the will. Who can prove by experience the nonexistence of a cause when all that experience teaches is that we do not perceive it? In such a case, however, the so-called moral imperative, which as such appears to be categorical and unconditional, would in fact be only a pragmatic precept that makes us attentive to our advantage and merely teaches us to take this into consideration.

4:420   We shall thus have to investigate entirely a priori the possibility of a *categorical* imperative, since we do not here have the advantage of its reality being given in experience, so that the possibility would be necessary not to establish it but merely to explain it.[z] In the meantime, however, we can see this much: that the categorical imperative alone has the tenor of[a] a practical **law**; all the others can indeed be called *principles* of the will but not laws, since what it is necessary to do merely for achieving a discretionary purpose can be regarded as in itself contingent and we can always be released from the precept if we give up the purpose; on the contrary, the unconditional command leaves the will no discretion[b] with respect to the opposite, so that it alone brings with it that necessity which we require of a law.

Second, in the case of this categorical imperative or law of morality the ground of the difficulty (of insight into its possibility) is also very great. It is an a priori synthetic practical proposition;[*] and since it is so difficult to see the possibility of this kind of proposition in theoretical cognition, it can be readily gathered that the difficulty will be no less in practical cognition.

In this task we want first to inquire whether the mere concept of a categorical imperative may not also provide its formula containing the

---

[*]I connect the deed with the will, without a presupposed condition from any inclination, a priori and hence necessarily (though only objectively, i.e., under the idea of a reason having complete control over all subjective motives).[c] This is, therefore, a practical proposition that does not derive the volition of an action analytically from another volition already presupposed (for we have no such perfect will), but connects it immediately with the concept of the will of a rational being as something that is not contained in it.

[z] *und also die Möglichkeit nicht zur Festsetzung, sondern bloss zur Erklärung nötig wäre*
[a] *als . . . laute*
[b] *dem Willen kein Belieben . . . frei läßt*
[c] *Bewegursachen*

30

proposition which alone can be a categorical imperative. For, how such an absolute command is possible, even if we know its tenor, will still require special and difficult toil, which, however, we postpone to the last section.

When I think of a *hypothetical* imperative in general I do not know beforehand what it will contain; I do not know this until I am given the condition. But when I think of a *categorical* imperative I know at once what it contains. For, since the imperative contains, beyond the law, only the necessity that the maxim* be in conformity with this law, while the law   4:421 contains no condition to which it would be limited, nothing is left with which the maxim of action is to conform but the universality of a law as such; and this conformity alone is what the imperative properly represents as necessary.

There is, therefore, only a single categorical imperative and it is this: *act only in accordance with that maxim through which you can at the same time will that it become a universal law.*

Now, if all imperatives of duty can be derived from this single imperative as from their principle, then, even though we leave it undecided whether what is called duty is not as such an empty concept, we shall at least be able to show what we think by it and what the concept wants to say.

Since the universality of law in accordance with which effects take place constitutes what is properly called *nature* in the most general sense (as regards its form) – that is, the existence of things insofar as it is determined in accordance with universal laws – the universal imperative of duty can also go as follows: *act as if the maxim of your action were to become by your will a* **universal law of nature.**

We shall now enumerate a few duties in accordance with the usual division of them into duties to ourselves and to other human beings and into perfect and imperfect duties.†

1) Someone feels sick of life because of a series of troubles that has grown to the point of despair, but is still so far in possession of his reason   4:422 that he can ask himself whether it would not be contrary to his duty to

---

*A *maxim* is the subjective principle of acting, and must be distinguished from the *objective* principle, namely the practical law. The former contains the practical rule determined by reason conformably with the conditions of the subject (often his ignorance or also his inclinations), and is therefore the principle in accordance with which the subject *acts;* but the law is the objective principle valid for every rational being, and the principle in accordance with which he *ought to act,* i.e., an imperative.

†It must be noted here that I reserve the division of duties entirely for a future *Metaphysics of Morals,* so that the division here stands only as one adopted at my discretion (for the sake of arranging my examples). For the rest, I understand here by a perfect duty one that admits no exception in favor of inclination, and then I have not merely external but also internal *perfect duties;* although this is contrary to the use of the word adopted in the schools, I do not intend to justify it here, since for my purpose it makes no difference whether or not it is granted me.

himself to take his own life. Now he inquires whether the maxim of his action could indeed become a universal law of nature. His maxim, however, is: from self-love I make it my principle to shorten my life when its longer duration threatens more troubles than it promises agreeableness. The only further question is whether this principle of self-love could become a universal law of nature. It is then seen at once that a nature whose law it would be to destroy life itself by means of the same feeling whose destination^d is to impel toward the furtherance of life would contradict itself and would therefore not subsist^e as nature; thus that maxim could not possibly be a law of nature and, accordingly, altogether opposes the supreme principle of all duty.

2) Another finds himself urged by need to borrow money. He well knows that he will not be able to repay it but sees also that nothing will be lent him unless he promises firmly to repay it within a determinate time. He would like to make such a promise, but he still has enough conscience to ask himself: is it not forbidden and contrary to duty to help oneself out of need in such a way? Supposing that he still decided to do so, his maxim of action would go as follows: when I believe myself to be in need of money I shall borrow money and promise to repay it, even though I know that this will never happen. Now this principle of self-love or personal advantage is perhaps quite consistent with my whole future welfare, but the question now is whether it is right. I therefore turn the demand of self-love into a universal law and put the question as follows: how would it be if my maxim became a universal law? I then see at once that it could never hold as a universal law of nature and be consistent with itself, but must necessarily contradict itself. For, the universality of a law that everyone, when he believes himself to be in need, could promise whatever he pleases with the intention of not keeping it would make the promise and the end one might have in it itself impossible, since no one would believe what was promised him but would laugh at all such expressions as vain pretenses.

3) A third finds in himself a talent that by means of some cultivation
4:423   could make him a human being useful for all sorts of purposes. However, he finds himself in comfortable circumstances and prefers to give himself up to pleasure than to trouble himself with enlarging and improving his fortunate natural predispositions.^{f} But he still asks himself whether his maxim of neglecting his natural gifts, besides being consistent with his propensity to amusement, is also consistent with what one calls duty. He now sees that a nature could indeed always subsist with such a universal law, although (as with the South Sea Islanders) the human being should

^{d} *Bestimmung*
^{e} *bestehen*
^{f} *Naturanlagen*

let his talents rust and be concerned with devoting his life merely to idleness, amusement, procreation – in a word, to enjoyment; only he cannot possibly **will** that this become a universal law or be put in us as such by means of natural instinct. For, as a rational being he necessarily wills that all the capacities in him be developed, since they serve him and are given to him for all sorts of possible purposes.

Yet a *fourth,* for whom things are going well while he sees that others (whom he could very well help) have to contend with great hardships, thinks: what is it to me? let each be as happy as heaven wills or as he can make himself; I shall take nothing from him nor even envy him; only I do not care to contribute anything to his welfare or to his assistance in need! Now, if such a way of thinking were to become a universal law the human race could admittedly very well subsist, no doubt even better than when everyone prates about sympathy and benevolence and even exerts himself to practice them occasionally, but on the other hand also cheats where he can, sells the right of human beings or otherwise infringes upon it. But although it is possible that a universal law of nature could very well subsist in accordance with such a maxim, it is still impossible to **will** that such a principle hold everywhere as a law of nature. For, a will that decided this would conflict with itself, since many cases could occur in which one would need the love and sympathy[g] of others and in which, by such a law of nature arisen from his own will, he would rob himself of all hope of the assistance he wishes for himself.

These are a few of the many actual duties, or at least of what we take to be such, whose derivation[h] from the one principle cited above is clear. We must *be able to will* that a maxim of our action become a universal law: this is the canon of moral appraisal of action in general. Some actions are so constituted that their maxim cannot even be *thought* without contradiction as a universal law of nature, far less could one *will* that it *should* become such. In the case of others that inner impossibility is indeed not to be found, but it is still impossible to *will* that their maxim be raised to the universality of a law of nature because such a will would contradict itself. It is easy to see that the first is opposed to strict or narrower (unremitting)[i] duty, the second only to wide (meritorious) duty; and so all duties, as far as the kind of obligation (not the object of their action) is concerned, have by these examples been set out completely in their dependence upon the one principle.

If we now attend to ourselves in any transgression of a duty, we find that we do not really will that our maxim should become a universal law, since that is impossible for us, but that the opposite of our maxim should

4:424

---

[g] *Teilnehmung*
[h] reading *Ableitung* instead of *Abteilung,* "classification"
[i] *unnachlaßlich*

33

instead remain a universal law, only we take the liberty of making an *exception* to it for ourselves (or just for this once) to the advantage of our inclination. Consequently, if we weighed all cases from one and the same point of view, namely that of reason, we would find a contradiction in our own will, namely that a certain principle be objectively necessary as a universal law and yet subjectively not hold universally but allow exceptions. Since, however, we at one time regard our action from the point of view of a will wholly conformed with reason but then regard the very same action from the point of view of a will affected by inclination, there is really no contradiction here but instead a resistance[j] of inclination to the precept of reason (*antagonismus*), through which the universality of the principle (*universalitas*) is changed into mere generality (*generalitas*) and the practical rational principle is to meet the maxim half way. Now, even though this cannot be justified in our own impartially rendered judgment, it still shows that we really acknowledge the validity of the categorical imperative and permit ourselves (with all respect for it) only a few exceptions that, as it seems to us, are inconsiderable and wrung from us.

4:425   We have therefore shown at least this much: that if duty is a concept that is to contain significance and real lawgiving for our actions it can be expressed only in categorical imperatives and by no means in hypothetical ones; we have also – and this is already a great deal – set forth distinctly and as determined for every use the content of the categorical imperative, which must contain the principle of all duty (if there is such a thing at all). But we have not yet advanced so far as to prove a priori that there really is such an imperative, that there is a practical law, which commands absolutely of itself and without any incentives, and that the observance of this law is duty.

For the purpose of achieving this it is of the utmost importance to take warning that we must not let ourselves think of wanting to derive the reality of this principle from the *special property of human nature*. For, duty is to be practical unconditional necessity of action and it must therefore hold for all rational beings (to which alone an imperative can apply at all) and *only because of this* be also a law for all human wills. On the other hand, what is derived from the special natural constitution of humanity – what is derived from certain feelings and propensities and even, if possible, from a special tendency that would be peculiar to human reason and would not have to hold necessarily for the will of every rational being – that can indeed yield a maxim for us but not a law; it can yield a subjective principle on which we might act if we have the propensity and inclination,[k] but not an objective principle on which we would be *directed* to act even though every propensity, inclination, and natural tendency of ours were

[j] *Widerstand*
[k] *nach welchem wir handeln zu dürfen Hang und Neigung haben*

against it – so much so that the sublimity and inner dignity of the command in a duty is all the more manifest the fewer are the subjective causes in favor of it and the more there are against it, without thereby weakening in the least the necessitation by the law or taking anything away from its validity.

Here, then, we see philosophy put in fact in a precarious position, which is to be firm even though there is nothing in heaven or on earth from which it depends or on which it is based. Here philosophy is to manifest its purity as sustainer of its own laws, not as herald of laws that an implanted sense or who knows what tutelary nature whispers to it, all of which – though they may always be better than nothing at all – can still never yield basic principles that reason dictates and that must have their   4:426
source entirely and completely a priori and, at the same time, must have their commanding authority from this: that they expect nothing from the inclination of human beings but everything from the supremacy of the law and the respect owed it or, failing this, condemn the human being to contempt for himself and inner abhorrence.

Hence everything empirical, as an addition *l* to the principle of morality, is not only quite inept for this; it is also highly prejudicial to the purity of morals, where the proper worth of an absolutely good will – a worth raised above all price – consists just in the principle of action being free from all influences of contingent grounds, which only experience can furnish. One cannot give too many or too frequent warnings against this laxity, or even mean cast of mind, which seeks its principle among empirical motives and laws; for, human reason in its weariness gladly rests on this pillow and in a dream of sweet illusions (which allow it to embrace a cloud instead of Juno) it substitutes for morality a bastard patched up from limbs of quite diverse ancestry, which looks like whatever one wants to see in it but not like virtue for him who has once seen virtue in her true form.*

The question is therefore this: is it a necessary law *for all rational beings* always to appraise their actions in accordance with such maxims as they themselves could will to serve as universal laws? If there is such a law, then it must already be connected (completely a priori) with the concept of the will of a rational being as such. But in order to discover this connection we must, however reluctantly, step forth, namely into metaphysics, although into a domain *m* of it that is distinct from speculative philosophy, namely   4:427

---

*To behold virtue in her proper form is nothing other than to present morality stripped of any admixture of the sensible and of any spurious adornments of reward or self-love. By means of the least effort of his reason everyone can easily become aware of how much virtue then eclipses everything else that appears charming to the inclinations, provided his reason is not altogether spoiled for abstraction.

l *Zutat*, literally "an ornament"
m *Gebiet*

into metaphysics of morals. In a practical philosophy, where we have to do not with assuming[n] grounds for what *happens* but rather laws for what *ought to happen* even if it never does, that is, objective practical laws, we do not need to undertake an investigation into the grounds on account of which something pleases or displeases; how the satisfaction of mere sensation differs from taste, and whether the latter differs from a general satisfaction of reason; upon what the feeling of pleasure or displeasure rests, and how from it desires and inclinations arise, and from them, with the cooperation of reason, maxims; for all that belongs to an empirical doctrine of the soul,[o] which would constitute the second part of the doctrine of nature when this is regarded as *philosophy of nature* insofar as it is based *on empirical laws*. Here, however, it is a question of objective practical laws and hence of the relation of a will to itself insofar as it determines itself only by reason; for then everything that has reference to the empirical falls away of itself, since if reason entirely by itself determines conduct (and the possibility of this is just what we want now to investigate), it must necessarily do so a priori.

The will is thought as a capacity to determine itself to acting in conformity with the *representation of certain laws*. And such a capacity can be found only in rational beings. Now, what serves the will as the objective ground of its self-determination is an end, and this, if it is given by reason alone, must hold equally for all rational beings. What, on the other hand, contains merely the ground of the possibility of an action the effect of which is an end is called a *means*. The subjective ground of desire is an *incentive*; the objective ground of volition is a *motive*; hence the distinction between subjective ends, which rest on incentives, and objective ends, which depend on motives, which hold for every rational being. Practical

4:428 principles are *formal* if they abstract from all subjective ends, whereas they are *material* if they have put these, and consequently certain incentives, at their basis. The ends that a rational being proposes at his discretion as *effects* of his actions (material ends) are all only relative; for only their mere relation to a specially constituted[p] faculty of desire on the part of the subject gives them their worth, which can therefore furnish no universal principles, no principles valid and necessary for all rational beings and also for every volition, that is, no practical laws. Hence all these relative ends are only the ground of hypothetical imperatives.

But suppose there were something the *existence of which in itself* has an absolute worth, something which as *an end in itself* could be a ground of determinate laws; then in it, and in it alone, would lie the ground of a possible categorical imperative, that is, of a practical law.

[n] *anzunehmen*
[o] *Seelenlehre*
[p] *geartetes*

Now I say that the human being and in general every rational being *exists* as an end in itself, *not merely as a means* to be used by this or that will at its discretion; instead he must in all his actions, whether directed to himself or also to other rational beings, always be regarded *at the same time as an end*. All objects of the inclinations have only a conditional worth; for, if there were not inclinations and the needs based on them, their object would be without worth. But the inclinations themselves, as sources of needs, are so far from having an absolute worth, so as to make one wish to have them,[q] that it must instead be the universal wish of every rational being to be altogether free from them. Thus the worth of any object *to be acquired* by our action is always conditional. Beings the existence of which rests not on our will but on nature, if they are beings without reason, still have only a relative worth, as means, and are therefore called *things*,[r] whereas rational beings are called *persons* because their nature already marks them out as an end in itself, that is, as something that may not be used merely as a means, and hence so far limits all choice (and is an object of respect). These, therefore, are not merely subjective ends, the existence of which as an effect of our action has a worth *for us*, but rather *objective ends*, that is, beings[s] the existence of which is in itself an end, and indeed one such that no other end, to which they would serve *merely* as means, can be put in its place, since without it nothing of *absolute worth* would be found anywhere; but if all worth were conditional and therefore contingent, then no supreme practical principle for reason could be found anywhere.

If, then, there is to be a supreme practical principle and, with respect to the human will, a categorical imperative, it must be one such that, from the representation of what is necessarily an end for everyone because it is an *end in itself*, it constitutes an *objective* principle of the will and thus can serve as a universal practical law.[t] The ground of this principle is: *rational nature exists as an end in itself*. The human being necessarily represents his own existence in this way; so far it is thus a *subjective* principle of human actions. But every other rational being also represents his existence in this way consequent on[u] just the same rational ground that also holds for me;* thus it is at the same time an *objective* principle from which, as a supreme

4:429

---

*Here I put forward this proposition as a postulate. The grounds for it will be found in the last Section.

[q] *um sie selbst zu wünschen*

[r] *Sachen*

[s] *Dinge.* Although both *Sache* and *Ding* would usually be translated as "thing," *Sache* has the technical sense of something usable that does not have free choice, i.e., "*Sache ist ein Ding*" to which nothing can be imputed (*The Metaphysics of Morals* 6:223).

[t] *ausmacht, mithin zum allgemeinen praktischen Gesetz dienen kann.* It is not clear, grammatically, whether the subject of "can serve" is "end in itself" or "objective principle."

[u] *zufolge*

practical ground, it must be possible to derive all laws of the will. The practical imperative will therefore be the following: *So act that you use humanity, whether in your own person or in the person of any other, always at the same time as an end, never merely as a means.* We shall see whether this can be carried out.

To keep to the preceding examples:

First, as regards the concept of necessary duty to oneself, someone who has suicide[v] in mind will ask himself whether his action can be consistent with the idea of humanity *as an end in itself.* If he destroys himself in order to escape from a trying condition he makes use of a person *merely as a means* to maintain a tolerable condition up to the end of life. A human being, however, is not a thing and hence not something that can be used *merely* as a means, but must in all his actions always be regarded as an end in itself. I cannot, therefore, dispose of a human being in my own person by maiming, damaging or killing him. (I must here pass over a closer determination of this principle that would prevent any misinterpretation, e.g., as to having limbs amputated in order to preserve myself, or putting my life in danger in order to preserve my life, and so forth; that belongs to morals proper.)

Second, as regards necessary duty to others or duty owed[w] them, he who has it in mind to make a false promise to others sees at once that he wants to make use of another human being *merely as a means,* without the other at the same time containing in himself the end. For, he whom I want to use for my purposes by such a promise cannot possibly agree to my way of behaving toward him, and so himself contain the end of this action. This conflict with the principle of other human beings is seen more distinctly if examples of assaults on the freedom and property of others are brought forward. For then it is obvious that he who transgresses the rights of human beings intends to make use of the person of others merely as means, without taking into consideration that, as rational beings, they are always to be valued at the same time as ends, that is, only as beings who must also be able to contain in themselves the end of the very same action.*

Third, with respect to contingent (meritorious) duty to oneself, it is not enough that the action does not conflict with humanity in our person as an

4:430

---

*Let it not be thought that the trite *quod tibi non vis fieri* etc.[x] can serve as norm or principle here. For it is, though with various limitations, only derived from the latter. It can be no universal law because it contains the ground neither of duties to oneself nor of duties of love to others (for many a man would gladly agree that others should not benefit him if only he might be excused from showing them beneficence), and finally it does not contain the ground of duties owed to others; for a criminal would argue on this ground against the judge punishing him, and so forth.

[v] *Selbstmorde,* perhaps "murdering himself." In *The Metaphysics of Morals, Selbstmord* (*homicidium dolosum*) is carefully distinguished from *Selbstentleibung* (*suicidium*) (6:421–4).

[w] *schuldige*

[x] what you do not want others to do to you, etc. [i.e., don't do the same to them]

end in itself; it must also *harmonize with it.* Now there are in humanity predispositions[y] to greater perfection, which belong to the end of nature with respect to humanity in our subject; to neglect these might admittedly be consistent with the *preservation* of humanity as an end in itself but not with the *furtherance* of this end.

Fourth, concerning meritorious duty to others, the natural end that all human beings have is their own happiness. Now, humanity might indeed subsist if no one contributed to the happiness of others but yet did not intentionally withdraw anything from it; but there is still only a negative and not a positive agreement with *humanity as an end in itself* unless everyone also tries, as far as he can, to further the ends of others. For, the ends of a subject who is an end in itself must as far as possible be also *my* ends, if that representation is to have its *full* effect in me.

This principle of humanity, and in general of every rational nature, *as an end in itself* (which is the supreme limiting condition of the freedom of action of every human being) is not borrowed from experience; first because of its universality, since it applies to all rational beings as such and no experience is sufficient to determine anything about them; second because in it humanity is represented not as an end of human beings (subjectively), that is, not as an object that we of ourselves actually make our end, but as an objective end that, whatever ends we may have, ought as law to constitute the supreme limiting condition of all subjective ends, so that the principle must arise from pure reason. That is to say, the ground of all practical lawgiving lies (in accordance with the first principle) *objectively in the rule* and the form of universality which makes it fit to be a law (possibly[z] a law of nature); *subjectively*, however, it lies in the *end;* but the subject of all ends is every rational being as an end in itself (in accordance with the second principle); from this there follows now the third practical principle of the will, as supreme condition of its harmony with universal practical reason, the idea *of the will of every rational being as a will giving universal law.* 4:431

In accordance with this principle all maxims are repudiated that are inconsistent with the will's own giving of universal law. Hence the will is not merely subject to the law but subject to it in such a way that it must be viewed as also giving the law to itself[a] and just because of this as first subject to the law (of which it can regard itself as the author).[b]

Imperatives as they were represented above – namely in terms of the conformity of actions with universal law similar to a *natural order* or of the universal *supremacy as ends[c]* of rational beings in themselves – did exclude

---

[y] *Anlagen*
[z] *allenfalls*
[a] Or "as itself lawgiving," *als selbstgesetzgebend*
[b] *Urheber*
[c] *Zweckvorzuges*

from their commanding authority any admixture of interest as incentive, just by their having been represented as categorical; but they were only *assumed*[d] to be categorical because we had to make such an assumption if we wanted to explain the concept of duty. But that there are practical propositions which command categorically could not itself be proved,[e] any more than it could be proved either here or anywhere else in this section; one thing, however, could still have been done: namely, to indicate in the imperative itself the renunciation of all interest, in volition from duty, by means of some determination the imperative contains, as the specific mark distinguishing[f] categorical from hypothetical imperatives; and this is done in the present third formula of the principle, namely the idea of the will of every rational being as a *will giving universal law.*

4:432

For when we think of a will of this kind, then although a will that *stands under law* may be bound to this law by means of some interest, a will that is itself the supreme lawgiver cannot possibly, as such, depend upon some interest; for, a will that is dependent in this way would itself need yet another law that would limit the interest of its self-love to the condition of a validity for universal law.

Thus the *principle* of every human will as *a will giving universal law through all its maxims,** provided it is otherwise correct, would be very *well suited* to be the categorical imperative by this: that just because of the idea of giving universal law *it is based on no interest* and therefore, among all possible imperatives, can alone be *unconditional;* or still better, by converting the proposition, if there is a categorical imperative (i.e., a law for every will of a rational being) it can only command that everything be done from the maxim of one's will as a will that could at the same time have as its object itself as giving universal law; for only then is the practical principle, and the imperative that the will obeys, unconditional, since it can have no interest as its basis.

If we look back upon all previous efforts that have ever been made to discover the principle of morality, we need not wonder now why all of them had to fail. It was seen that the human being is bound to laws by his duty, but it never occurred to them that he is subject *only to laws given by himself but still universal* and that he is bound only to act in conformity with his own will, which, however, in accordance with nature's end[g] is a will giving universal law. For, if one thought of him only as subject to a law (whatever it may be), this law had to carry with it some interest by way of

4:433

---

*I may be excused from citing examples to illustrate this principle, since those that have already illustrated the categorical imperative and its formula can all serve for the same end here.

[d] *angenommen*

[e] *bewiesen werden*

[f] *Unterscheidungszeichen*

[g] *dem Naturzwecke nach*

attraction or constraint, since it did not as a law arise from *his* will; in order to conform with the law, his will had instead to be constrained by *something else* to act in a certain way.[h] By this quite necessary consequence, however, all the labor to find a supreme ground of duty was irretrievably lost. For, one never arrived at duty but instead at the necessity of an action from a certain interest. This might be one's own or another's interest. But then the imperative had to turn out always conditional and could not be fit for a moral command. I will therefore call this basic principle the principle of the **autonomy** of the will in contrast with every other, which I accordingly count as **heteronomy**.

The concept of every rational being as one who must regard himself as giving universal law through all the maxims of his will, so as to appraise himself and his actions from this point of view, leads to a very fruitful concept dependent upon it,[i] namely that *of a kingdom*[j] *of ends.*

By a *kingdom* I understand a systematic union of various rational beings through common laws. Now since laws determine ends in terms of their universal validity, if we abstract from the personal differences of rational beings as well as from all the content of their private ends we shall be able to think of a whole of all ends in systematic connection (a whole both of rational beings as ends in themselves and of the ends of his own that each may set himself), that is, a kingdom of ends, which is possible in accordance with the above principles.

For, all rational beings stand under the *law* that each of them is to treat himself and all others *never merely as means* but always *at the same time as ends in themselves.* But from this there arises a systematic union of rational beings through common objective laws, that is, a kingdom, which can be called a kingdom of ends (admittedly only an ideal) because what these laws have as their purpose is just the relation of these beings to one another as ends and means.

A rational being belongs as a *member* to the kingdom of ends when he gives universal laws in it but is also himself subject to these laws. He belongs to it *as sovereign*[k] when, as lawgiving, he is not subject to the will of any other.

A rational being must always regard himself as lawgiving in a kingdom of ends possible through freedom of the will, whether as a member or as sovereign. He cannot, however, hold the position of sovereign merely by the maxims of his will but only in case he is a completely independent being, without needs and with unlimited resources[l] adequate to his will.   4:434

---

[h] *sondern dieser gesetzmässig von etwas anderm genötigt wurde, auf gewisse Weise zu handeln*
[i] Or "attached to it," *ihm anhangenden*
[j] *Reich,* which could also be translated "commonwealth"
[k] *als Oberhaupt*
[l] *Vermögen*

Morality consists, then, in the reference of all action to the lawgiving by which alone a kingdom of ends is possible. This lawgiving must, however, be found in every rational being himself and be able to arise from his will, the principle of which is, accordingly: to do no action on any other maxim than one such that it would be consistent with it to be a universal law, and hence to act only *so that the will could regard itself as at the same time giving universal law through its maxim.* Now, if maxims are not already of their nature in agreement with this objective principle of rational beings as givers of universal law, the necessity of an action in accordance with this principle is called practical necessitation, that is, *duty.* Duty does not apply to the sovereign in the kingdom of ends, but it does apply to every member of it and indeed to all in equal measure.

The practical necessity of acting in accordance with this principle, that is, duty, does not rest at all on feelings, impulses, and inclinations but merely on the relation of rational beings to one another, in which the will of a rational being must always be regarded as at the same time *lawgiving,* since otherwise it could not be thought as an *end in itself.* Reason accordingly refers every maxim of the will as giving universal law to every other will and also to every action toward oneself, and does so not for the sake of any other practical motive or any future advantage but from the idea of the *dignity* of a rational being, who obeys no law other than that which he himself at the same time gives.

In the kingdom of ends everything has either a *price* or a *dignity.*[m] What has a price can be replaced by something else as its *equivalent*; what on the other hand is raised above all price and therefore admits of no equivalent has a dignity.

4:435 What is related to general human inclinations and needs has a *market price*; that which, even without presupposing a need, conforms with a certain taste, that is, with a delight[n] in the mere purposeless[o] play of our mental powers, has a *fancy price*;[p] but that which constitutes the condition under which alone something can be an end in itself has not merely a relative worth, that is, a price, but an inner worth, that is, *dignity.*

Now, morality is the condition under which alone a rational being can be an end in itself, since only through this is it possible to be a lawgiving member in the kingdom of ends. Hence morality, and humanity insofar as it is capable of morality, is that which alone has dignity. Skill and diligence in work have a market price; wit, lively imagination and humor have a fancy price; on the other hand, fidelity in promises and benevolence from basic principles (not from instinct) have an inner worth. Nature, as well as

[m] *Würde*
[n] *Wohlgefallen*
[o] *zwecklosen*
[p] *Affectionspreis*

art, contains nothing that, lacking these, it could put in their place; for their worth does not consist in the effects arising from them, in the advantage and use they provide, but in dispositions,*q* that is, in maxims of the will that in this way are ready to manifest themselves through actions, even if success does not favor them. Such actions also need no recommendation from any subjective disposition*r* or taste, so as to be looked upon with immediate favor and delight, nor do they need any immediate propensity or feeling for them; they present the will that practices them as the object of an immediate respect, and nothing but reason is required to *impose* them upon the will, not to *coax* them from it, which latter would in any case be a contradiction in the case of duties. This estimation therefore lets the worth of such a cast of mind be cognized as dignity and puts it infinitely above all price, with which it cannot be brought into comparison or competition at all without, as it were, assaulting its holiness.*s*

And what is it, then, that justifies a morally good disposition, or virtue, in making such high claims? It is nothing less than the *share* it affords a rational being *in the giving of universal laws*, by which it makes him fit to be a member of a possible kingdom of ends, which he was already destined to be by his own nature as an end in itself and, for that very reason, as lawgiving in the kingdom of ends – as free with respect to all laws of nature, obeying only those which he himself gives and in accordance with which his maxims can belong to a giving of universal law (to which at the same time he subjects himself). For, nothing can have a worth other than that which the law determines for it. But the lawgiving itself, which determines all worth, must for that very reason have a dignity, that is, an unconditional, incomparable worth; and the word *respect* alone provides a becoming expression for the estimate of it that a rational being must give. *Autonomy* is therefore the ground of the dignity of human nature and of every rational nature.

4:436

The above three ways of representing the principle of morality are at bottom only so many formulae of the very same law, and any one of them of itself unites the other two in it. There is nevertheless a difference among them, which is indeed subjectively rather than objectively practical, intended namely to bring an idea of reason closer to intuition (by a certain analogy) and thereby to feeling. All maxims have, namely,

1) a *form*, which consists in universality; and in this respect the formula of the moral imperative is expressed thus: that maxims must be chosen*t* as if they were to hold as universal laws of nature;

2) a *matter*, namely an end, and in this respect the formula says that a

---

q *Gesinnungen*
r *Disposition*
s *Heiligkeit*
t *so müssen gewählt werden*

rational being, as an end by its nature and hence as an end in itself, must in every maxim serve as the limiting condition of all merely relative and arbitrary" ends;

3) *a complete determination* of all maxims by means of that formula, namely that all maxims from one's own lawgiving are to harmonize with a possible kingdom of ends as with a kingdom of nature.* A progression takes place here, as through the categories of the *unity* of the form of the will (its universality), the *plurality* of the matter (of objects, i.e., of ends), and the *allness*ᵛ or totality of the system of these. But one does better always to proceed in moral *appraisal* by the strict method and put at its basis the universal formula of the categorical imperative: *act in accordance with a maxim that can at the same time make itself a universal law.* If, however, one wants also to provide *access* for the moral law, it is very useful to bring one and the same action under the three concepts mentioned above and thereby, as far as possible, bring it closer to intuition.

4:437

We can now end where we set out from at the beginning, namely with the concept of a will unconditionally good. *That will is absolutely good* which cannot be evil, hence whose maxim, if made a universal law, can never conflict with itself. This principle is, accordingly, also its supreme law: act always on that maxim whose universality as a law you can at the same time will; this is the sole condition under which a will can never be in conflict with itself, and such an imperative is categorical. Since the validity of the will as a universal law for possible actions has an analogy with the universal connection of the existence of things in accordance with universal laws, which is the formal aspect of nature in general, the categorical imperative can also be expressed thus: *act in accordance with maxims that can at the same time have as their object themselves as universal laws of nature.* In this way, then, the formula of an absolutely good will is provided.

Rational nature is distinguished from the rest of nature by this, that it sets itself an end. This end would be the matter of every good will. But since, in the idea of a will absolutely good without any limiting condition (attainment of this or that end) abstraction must be made altogether from every end to be *effected* (this would make every will only relatively good), the end must here be thought not as an end to be effected but as an *independently existing*ʷ end, and hence thought only negatively, that is, as

---

Teleology considers nature as a kingdom of ends, *morals* considers a possible kingdom of ends as a kingdom of nature. In the former the kingdom of ends is a theoretical idea for explaining what exists. In the latter, it is a practical idea for the sake of bringing about, in conformity with this very idea, that which does not exist but which can become real by means of our conduct.

" *willkürlichen*
ᵛ *Allheit*
ʷ *selbstständiger*

that which must never be acted against and which must therefore in every volition be estimated never merely as a means but always at the same time as an end. Now, this end can be nothing other than the subject of all possible ends itself, because this subject is also the subject of a possible absolutely good will; for, such a will cannot without contradiction be subordinated to any other object. The principle, so act with reference to every rational being (yourself and others) that in your maxim it holds at the same time as an end in itself, is thus at bottom the same as the basic principle, act on a maxim that at the same time contains in itself its own universal validity for every rational being. For, to say that in the use of means to any end I am to limit my maxim to the condition of its universal validity as a law for every subject is tantamount to saying that the subject of ends, that is, the rational being itself, must be made the basis of all maxims of actions, never merely as a means but as the supreme limiting condition in the use of all means, that is, always at the same time as an end. 4:438

Now, from this it follows incontestably that every rational being, as an end in itself, must be able to regard himself as also giving universal laws with respect to any law whatsoever to which he may be subject; for, it is just this fitness of his maxims for giving universal law that marks him out as an end in itself; it also follows that this dignity (prerogative) he has over all merely natural beings brings with it that he must always take his maxims from the point of view of himself, and likewise every other rational being, as lawgiving beings (who for this reason are also called persons). Now in this way a world of rational beings (*mundus intelligibilis*)^x as a kingdom of ends is possible, through the giving of their own laws^y by all persons as members. Consequently, every rational being must act as if he were by his maxims at all times a lawgiving member of the universal kingdom of ends. The formal principle of these maxims is, act as if your maxims were to serve at the same time as a universal law (for all rational beings). A kingdom of ends is thus possible only by analogy with a kingdom of nature; the former, however, is possible only through maxims, that is, rules imposed upon oneself, the latter only through laws of externally necessitated efficient causes. Despite this, nature as a whole, even though it is regarded as a machine, is still given the name "a kingdom of nature" insofar as and because it has reference to rational beings as its ends. Now, such a kingdom of ends would actually come into existence through maxims whose rule the categorical imperative prescribes to all rational beings *if they were universally followed.* It is true that, even though a rational being scrupulously follows this maxim himself, he cannot for that reason

---

^x intelligible world
^y *durch die eigene Gesetzgebung*

4:439

count upon every other to be faithful to the same maxim nor can he count upon the kingdom of nature and its purposive order to harmonize with him, as a fitting member, toward a kingdom of ends possible through himself, that is, upon its favoring his expectation of happiness; nevertheless that law, act in accordance with the maxims of a member giving universal laws for a merely possible kingdom of ends, remains in its full force because it commands categorically. And just in this lies the paradox that the mere dignity of humanity as rational nature, without any other end or advantage to be attained by it – hence respect for a mere idea – is yet to serve as an inflexible precept of the will, and that it is just in this independence of maxims from all such incentives that their sublimity consists, and the worthiness of every rational subject to be a lawgiving member in the kingdom of ends; for otherwise he would have to be represented only as subject to the natural law of his needs. Even if the kingdom of nature as well as the kingdom of ends were thought as united under one sovereign, so that the latter would no longer remain a mere idea but would obtain true reality, it would no doubt gain the increment of a strong incentive but never any increase of its inner worth; for, even this sole absolute lawgiver would, despite this, still have to be represented as appraising the worth of rational beings only by their disinterested conduct, prescribed to themselves merely from that idea. The essence of things is not changed by their external relations; and that which, without taking account of such relations, alone constitutes the worth of a human being is that in terms of which he must also be appraised by whoever does it, even by the supreme being. *Morality* is thus the relation of actions to the autonomy of the will, that is, to a possible giving of universal law through its maxims. An action that can coexist with the autonomy of the will is *permitted;* one that does not accord with it is *forbidden.* A will whose maxims necessarily harmonize with the laws of autonomy is a *holy,* absolutely good will. The dependence upon the principle of autonomy of a will that is not absolutely good (moral necessitation) is *obligation.* This, accordingly, cannot be attributed to a holy being. The objective necessity of an action from obligation is called *duty.*

From what has just been said it is now easy to explain how it happens that, although in thinking the concept of duty we think of subjection to the law, yet at the same time we thereby represent a certain sublimity and *dignity* in the person who fulfills all his duties. For there is indeed no sublimity in him insofar as he is *subject* to the moral law, but there certainly is insofar as he is at the same time *lawgiving* with respect to it and only for that reason subordinated to it. We have also shown above how neither fear nor inclination but simply respect for the law is that incentive which can give actions a moral worth. Our own will insofar as it would act only under the condition of a possible giving of universal law through its maxims – this will possible for us in idea – is the proper object of respect; and the

4:440

dignity of humanity consists just in this capacity to give universal law, though with the condition of also being itself subject to this very lawgiving.

AUTONOMY OF THE WILL
AS THE SUPREME PRINCIPLE OF MORALITY

Autonomy of the will is the property[a] of the will by which it is a law to itself (independently of any property of the objects of volition). The principle of autonomy is, therefore: to choose only in such a way that the maxims of your choice[b] are also included[c] as universal law in the same volition. That this practical rule is an imperative, that is, that the will of every rational being is necessarily bound to it as a condition, cannot be proved by mere analysis[d] of the concepts to be found in it, because it is a synthetic proposition; one would have to go beyond cognition of objects to a critique of the subject, that is, of pure practical reason, since this synthetic proposition, which commands apodictically, must be capable of being cognized completely a priori. This business, however, does not belong in the present section. But that the above principle of autonomy is the sole principle of morals can well be shown by mere analysis of the concepts of morality. For, by this analysis we find that its principle must be a categorical imperative, while this commands neither more nor less than just this autonomy.

HETERONOMY OF THE WILL 4:441
AS THE SOURCE OF ALL SPURIOUS PRINCIPLES OF MORALITY

If the will seeks the law that is to determine it *anywhere else* than in the fitness of its maxims for its own giving of universal law – consequently if, in going beyond itself, it seeks this law in a property of any of its objects – *heteronomy* always results. The will in that case does not give itself the law; instead the object, by means of its relation to the will, gives the law to it. This relation, whether it rests upon inclination or upon representations of reason, lets only hypothetical imperatives become possible: I ought to do something *because I will something else.* On the contrary, the moral and therefore categorical imperative says: I ought to act in such or such a way even though I have not willed anything else. For example, the former says: I ought not to lie if I will to keep my reputation; but the latter says: I ought

---

[a] *Beschaffenheit*
[b] *zu wählen also so, dass die Maximen seiner Wahl.* Kant has apparently not yet drawn the distinction between *Wille* ("the will") and *Willkür* ("choice" or "the power of choice") so prominent in *The Metaphysics of Morals.*
[c] *mit begriffen seien*
[d] *Zergliederung*

not to lie even though it would not bring me the least discredit. The latter must therefore abstract from all objects to this extent: that they have no *influence* at all on the will, so that practical reason (the will) may not merely administer an interest not belonging to it,*ᵉ* but may simply show its own commanding authority as supreme lawgiving. Thus, for example, I ought to try to further the happiness of others, not as if its existence were of any consequence to me (whether because of immediate inclination or because of some indirect agreeableness through reason), but simply because a maxim that excludes this cannot be included as a universal law in one and the same volition.

DIVISION
OF ALL POSSIBLE PRINCIPLES OF MORALITY
TAKEN FROM
HETERONOMY ASSUMED AS THE
BASIC CONCEPT

Here, as everywhere else, human reason in its pure use, as long as it lacks a critique, first tries all possible wrong ways before it succeeds in finding the only true way.

4:442   All principles that can be taken from this point of view are either *empirical* or *rational*. The **first**, taken from the principle of *happiness*, are built upon physical or moral feeling; the second, taken from the principle of *perfection*, are built either upon the rational concept of perfection as a possible effect of our will or upon the concept of an independently existing perfection (the will of God) as the determining cause of our will.

Empirical principles are not at all fit to be the ground of moral laws. For, the universality with which these are to hold for all rational beings without distinction – the unconditional practical necessity which is thereby imposed upon them – comes to nothing if their ground is taken from the *special constitution of human nature* or the contingent circumstances in which it is placed. The principle of *one's own happiness*, however, is the most objectionable, not merely because it is false and experience contradicts the pretense that well-being always proportions itself to good conduct, nor yet merely because it contributes nothing at all to the establishment of morality, since making someone happy is quite different from making him good, or making him prudent and sharp-sighted for his own advantage is quite different from making him virtuous; it is the most objectionable because it bases morality on incentives that undermine it and destroy all its sublimity, since they put motives to virtue and those to vice in one class and only teach us to calculate better, but quite obliterate

---

ᵉ fremdes Interesse. Fremd is also translated as "alien," "foreign," or "another's."

the specific difference between virtue and vice. On the other hand, moral feeling – this supposed special sense* (however superficial the appeal to it is, inasmuch as those who cannot *think* believe they can help themselves out by feeling in what has to do merely with universal law,*f* and however little feelings, which by nature differ infinitely from one another in degree, can furnish a uniform standard of good and evil, and one cannot judge validly for others by means of one's feeling) – nevertheless remains closer to morality and its dignity inasmuch as it shows virtue the honor of ascribing to her *immediately* the delight*g* and esteem we have for her and does not, as it were, tell her to her face that it is not her beauty but only our advantage that attaches us to her.

4:443

Among the *rational* grounds of morality or those based on reason,*h* the ontological concept of *perfection* (however empty, however indeterminate and hence useless it is for finding, in the immeasurable field of possible reality, the greatest sum appropriate to us; and however much, in trying to distinguish specifically the reality here in question from every other, it has an unavoidable propensity to get involved in a circle and cannot avoid covertly presupposing the morality which it is supposed to explain) is nevertheless better than the theological concept, which derives morality from a divine, all-perfect will; it is better not merely because we cannot intuit the perfection of this will but can only derive it from our concepts, among which that of morality is foremost, but because if we do not do this (and to do it would be a grossly circular explanation), the concept of his will still left to us, made up of the attributes*i* of desire for glory and dominion combined with dreadful representations of power and vengefulness, would have to be the foundation for a system of morals that would be directly opposed to morality.

But if I had to choose between the concept of the moral sense and that of perfection generally (both of which at least do not infringe upon morality, even though they are not at all fit to support it as its foundation), then I should decide*j* for the latter; for, since it at least withdraws the decision of the question from sensibility and brings it to the court of pure reason,

---

*I count the principle of moral feeling under that of happiness because every empirical interest promises to contribute to our well-being by the agreeableness that something affords, whether this happens immediately and without a view to advantage or with regard for it. One must likewise, with Hutcheson,[6] count the principle of sympathy with the happiness of others under the moral sense assumed by him.

f It is not altogether clear whether the clause "in what has to do merely with universal law" modifies "think" or "feeling."

g *Wohlgefallen*

h *Unter den rationalen oder Vernunftgründen*

i *Eigenschaften*

j *bestimmen*

even though it decides nothing there it still preserves the indeterminate idea (of a will good in itself) unfalsified, for closer determination.

For the rest, I believe I may be excused from a lengthy refutation of all these doctrines.[k] That is so easy, and is presumably so well seen even by those whose office requires them to declare themselves for one of these theories (because their hearers would not tolerate suspension of judgment), that it would be merely superfluous labor. But what interests us more here is to know that all these principles set up nothing other than heteronomy of the will as the first ground of morality, and just because of this they must necessarily fail in their end.

4:444 Wherever an object of the will has to be laid down as the basis for prescribing the rule that determines the will, there the rule is none other than heteronomy; the imperative is conditional, namely: *if* or *because* one wills this object, one ought to act in such or such a way; hence it can never command morally, that is, categorically. Whether the object determines the will by means of inclination, as in the principle of one's own happiness, or by means of reason directed to objects of our possible volition in general, as in the principle of perfection, the will never determines itself *immediately*, just by the representation of an action, but only by means of an incentive that the anticipated effect of the action has upon the will: *I ought to do something on this account, that I will something else*, and here yet another law must be put as a basis in me, the subject, in accordance with which I necessarily will this something else, which law in turn needs an imperative that would limit this maxim. For, because the impulse that the representation of an object possible through our powers is to exert on the will of the subject in accordance with his natural constitution belongs to the nature of the subject – whether to his sensibility (inclination and taste) or to his understanding and reason, which by the special constitution of their nature employ themselves with delight[l] upon an object – it would, strictly speaking, be nature that gives the law; and this, as a law of nature, must not only be cognized and proved by experience – and is therefore in itself contingent and hence unfit for an apodictic practical rule, such as moral rules must be – but it is *always only heteronomy* of the will; the will would not give itself the law but a foreign impulse would give the law to it by means of the subject's nature, which is attuned to be receptive to it.

An absolutely good will, whose principle must be a categorical imperative, will therefore, indeterminate with respect to all objects, contain merely the *form* of *volition* as such and indeed as autonomy; that is, the fitness of the maxims of every good will to make themselves into universal law is itself the sole law that the will of every rational being imposes upon

[k] *Lehrbegriffe*
[l] *Wohlgefallen*

itself, without having to put underneath it some incentive or interest as a basis.

How such a synthetic practical proposition is possible a priori and why it is necessary is a problem whose solution does not lie within the bounds of metaphysics of morals, and we have not here affirmed its truth, much less pretended to have a proof of it in our power. By explicating the generally 4:445 received concept of morality we showed only that an autonomy of the will unavoidably depends upon it,*m* or much rather lies at its basis. Thus whoever holds morality to be something and not a chimerical idea without any truth must also admit the principle of morality brought forward. This section then, like the first, was merely analytic. That morality is no phantom – and this follows if the categorical imperative, and with it the autonomy of the will, is true and absolutely necessary as an a priori principle – requires a possible *synthetic use of pure practical reason,* which use, however, we cannot venture upon without prefacing it by a *critique* of this rational faculty itself, the main features of which we have to present, sufficiently for our purpose, in the last section.

m anhänge, perhaps "is attached to it"

Section III
Transition from metaphysics of morals to the critique of pure practical reason

THE CONCEPT OF FREEDOM IS THE KEY TO THE EXPLANATIONⁿ OF THE AUTONOMY OF THE WILL

Will is a kind of causality of living beings insofar as they are rational, and *freedom* would be that property^o of such causality that it can be efficient independently of alien causes *determining* it, just as *natural necessity* is the property of the causality of all nonrational beings to be determined to activity by the influence of alien causes.

The preceding definition^p of freedom is *negative* and therefore unfruitful for insight into^q its essence; but there flows from it a *positive* concept of freedom, which is so much the richer and more fruitful. Since the concept of causality brings with it that of laws in accordance with which, by something that we call a cause, something else, namely an effect, must be posited, so freedom, although it is not a property of the will in accordance with natural laws, is not for that reason lawless but must instead be a causality in accordance with immutable laws but of a special kind; for otherwise a free will would be an absurdity.^r Natural necessity was a heteronomy of efficient causes, since every effect was possible only in accordance with the law that something else determines the efficient cause to causality; what, then, can freedom of the will be other than autonomy, that is, the will's property of being a law to itself? But the proposition, the will is in all its actions a law to itself, indicates only the principle, to act on no other maxim than that which can also have as object itself as a universal law. This, however, is precisely the formula of the

4:447 (margin)

ⁿ *Erklärung*
^o *Eigenschaft*
^p *Erklärung.* On the translation of *Erklärung* see *The Metaphysics of Morals* (6:226).
^q *einzusehen.* As was noted above, Kant seems on the whole to use *einsehen* informally. In the Jäsche *Logik* (9: 64–5), however, he distinguishes seven levels of *Erkenntnis* in the general sense, the sixth of which is *einsehen (perspicere)*, i.e., to cognize through reason or a priori, and the seventh *begreifen (comprehendere)*, which adds to *einsehen* "sufficiently for our purpose." Some passages in Section III, notably 4:459 and 460, suggest that he has this distinction in mind.
^r *Unding*

categorical imperative and is the principle of morality; hence a free will and a will under moral laws are one and the same.

If, therefore, freedom of the will is presupposed, morality together with its principle follows from it by mere analysis of its concept. But the principle of morality – that an absolutely good will is that whose maxim can always contain itself regarded as a universal law – is nevertheless always a synthetic proposition; for, by analysis of the concept of an absolutely good will that property of its maxim cannot be discovered. Such synthetic propositions are possible only in this way: that the two cognitions are bound together* by their connection with a third in which they are both to be found. The *positive* concept of freedom provides this third cognition, which cannot be, as in the case of physical causes, the nature of the sensible world (in the concept of which the concepts of something as cause in relation to *something else* as effect come together). What this third cognition is, to which freedom points us and of which we have an idea a priori, cannot yet be shown here and now; nor can the deduction of the concept of freedom from pure practical reason, and with it the possibility of a categorical imperative as well, as yet be made comprehensible; instead, some further preparation is required.

FREEDOM MUST BE PRESUPPOSED AS A PROPERTY OF THE WILL OF ALL RATIONAL BEINGS

It is not enough that we ascribe freedom to our will on whatever ground, if we do not have sufficient ground for attributing it also to all rational beings. For, since morality serves as a law for us only as rational beings, it must also hold for all rational beings; and since it must be derived solely from the property of freedom, freedom must also be proved* as a property of all rational beings; and it is not enough to demonstrate* it from certain supposed experiences of human nature (though this is also absolutely impossible and it can be demonstrated only a priori), but it must be proved as belonging to the activity of all beings whatever that are rational and endowed with a will. I say now: every being that cannot act otherwise than *under the idea of freedom* is just because of that really free in a practical respect, that is, all laws that are inseparably bound up with freedom hold for him just as if his will had been validly pronounced* free also in itself and in theoretical philosophy.* Now I assert that to every rational being

4:448

---

* *untereinander verbunden werden*
* *bewiesen*
* *darzutun*
* *gültig für frei erklärt würde*
*I follow this route – that of assuming freedom, sufficiently for our purpose, only as laid down by rational beings merely *in idea* as a ground for their actions – so that I need not be

having a will we must necessarily lend the idea of freedom also, under which alone he acts. For in such a being we think of a reason that is practical, that is, has causality with respect to its objects. Now, one cannot possibly think of a reason that would consciously receive direction from any other quarter with respect to its judgments, since the subject would then attribute the determination of his judgment not to his reason but to an impulse. Reason must regard itself as the author of its principles independently of alien influences; consequently, as practical reason or as the will of a rational being it must be regarded of itself as free, that is, the will of such a being cannot be a will of his own except under the idea of freedom, and such a will must in a practical respect^x thus be attributed to every rational being.

OF THE INTEREST ATTACHING ^{y} TO THE IDEAS OF MORALITY

We have finally traced the determinate concept of morality back to the idea of freedom; but we could not even prove the latter as something real in ourselves and in human nature; we saw only that we must presuppose it if we want to think of a being as rational and endowed with consciousness of his causality with respect to actions, that is, with a will, and so we find that on just the same grounds we must assign to every being endowed with reason and will this property of determining himself to action under the idea of his freedom.

4:449

But there also flowed from the presupposition of this idea consciousness of a law for acting: that subjective principles of actions, that is, maxims, must always be so adopted that they can also hold as objective, that is, hold universally as principles, and so serve for our own giving of universal laws. But why, then, ought I to subject myself to this principle and do so simply as a rational being, thus also subjecting to it all other beings endowed with reason? I am willing to admit that no interest *impels* me to do so, for that would not give a categorical imperative; but I must still necessarily *take* an interest in it and have insight into how this comes about; for this "ought" is strictly speaking a "will"^{z} that holds for every rational being under the condition that reason in him is practical without hindrance; but for beings

bound to prove freedom in its theoretical respect^w as well. For even if the latter is left unsettled, still the same laws hold for a being that cannot act otherwise than under the idea of its own freedom as would bind a being that was actually free. Thus we can escape here from the burden that weighs upon theory.

^{w} *Absicht*

^{x} *in praktischer Absicht.* The subject of "must be attributed" could be either "this idea" or "such a will."

^{y} *welches den Ideen . . . anhängt*

^{z} *dieses Sollen ist eigentlich ein Wollen*

like us – who are also affected by sensibility, by incentives of a different kind, and in whose case that which reason by itself would do is not always done – that necessity of action is called only an "ought," and the subjective necessity is distinguished from the objective.

It seems, then, that in the idea of freedom we have actually only presupposed the moral law, namely the principle of the autonomy of the will itself, and could not prove by itself its reality and objective necessity; and in that case we should still have gained something considerable by at least determining the genuine principle more accurately than had previously been done, but we should have got no further with respect to its validity and the practical necessity of subjecting oneself to it; for, if someone asked us why the universal validity of our maxim as a law must be the limiting condition of our actions, and on what we base the worth we assign to this way of acting – a worth so great that there can be no higher interest anywhere – and asked us how it happens that a human being believes that only through this does he feel his personal worth, in comparison with which that of an agreeable or disagreeable condition^a is to be held as nothing, we could give him no satisfactory answer.

4:450

We do indeed find that we can take an interest in a personal characteristic^b that brings with it no interest at all in a condition, if only the former makes us fit to participate in the latter in case reason were to effect the distribution, that is, that mere worthiness to be happy, even without the motive of participating in this happiness, can interest us of itself; but this judgment is in fact only the result of the importance we have already supposed belongs to the moral law (when by the idea of freedom we detach ourselves from all empirical interest); but we cannot yet see, in this way, that we ought to detach ourselves from such interest, that is, to regard ourselves as free in acting and so to hold ourselves yet subject to certain laws in order to find merely in our own person a worth that can compensate us for the loss of everything that provides a worth to our condition; and we cannot yet see how this is possible, and hence *on what grounds^c the moral law is binding.*

It must be freely admitted that a kind of circle comes to light here from which, as it seems, there is no way to escape. We take ourselves as free in the order of efficient causes in order to think ourselves under moral laws in the order of ends; and we afterwards think ourselves as subject to these laws because we have ascribed to ourselves freedom of will: for, freedom and the will's own lawgiving are both autonomy and hence reciprocal concepts, and for this very reason one cannot be used to explain the other or to furnish a ground for it but can at most be used only for the logical

---

^{a} *Zustand*
^{b} *Beschaffenheit*
^{c} *woher*

purpose of reducing apparently different representations of the same object to one single concept (as different fractions of equal value are reduced to their lowest expression).

One resource, however, still remains to us, namely to inquire whether we do not take a different standpoint when by means of freedom we think of ourselves as causes efficient a priori than when we represent ourselves in terms of our actions as effects that we see before our eyes.

No subtle reflection is required to make the following remark, and one may assume that the commonest understanding can make it, though in its own way, by an obscure discrimination of judgment which it calls feeling: that all representations which come to us involuntarily^d (as do those of the senses) enable us to cognize objects only as they affect us and we remain ignorant of what they may be in themselves so that, as regards representations of this kind, even with the most strenuous attentiveness and distinctness that the understanding can ever bring to them we can achieve only cognition *of appearances*, never of *things in themselves*. As soon as this distinction has once been made (perhaps merely by means of the difference noticed between representations given us from somewhere else and in which we are passive, and those that we produce simply from ourselves and in which we show our activity), then it follows of itself that we must admit and assume behind appearances something else that is not appearance, namely things in themselves, although, since we can never become acquainted with them but only with how they affect us, we resign ourselves to being unable to come any closer to them or ever to know what they are in themselves. This must yield a distinction, although a crude one, between a *world of sense* and the *world of understanding,* the first of which can be very different according to the difference of sensibility in various observers of the world while the second, which is its basis, always remains the same. Even as to himself, the human being cannot claim to cognize what he is in himself through the cognizance he has by inner sensation. For, since he does not as it were create himself and does not get his concept a priori but empirically, it is natural that he can obtain information even about himself only through inner sense and so only through the appearance of his nature and the way in which his consciousness is affected – although beyond this constitution of his own subject, made up of nothing but appearances, he must necessarily assume something else lying at their basis, namely his ego as it may be constituted in itself; and thus as regards mere perception and receptivity to sensations he must count himself as belonging to the *world of sense,* but with regard to what there may be of pure activity in him (what reaches consciousness immediately and not through affection of the senses) he must count himself as belonging to the *intellectual world,* of which however he has no further cognizance.

^{d} *ohne unsere Willkür*

4:451

A reflective human being must come to a conclusion of this kind about all the things that present themselves to him; presumably it is also to be found even in the most common understanding, which, as is well known, is very much inclined to expect behind the objects of the senses something else invisible and active of itself – but it spoils this again by quickly making this invisible something sensible in turn, that is, wanting to make it an object of intuition, so that it does not thereby become any the wiser.

4:452

Now, a human being really finds in himself a capacity by which he distinguishes himself from all other things, even from himself insofar as he is affected by objects, and that is *reason*. This, as pure self-activity, is raised even above the *understanding* by this: that though the latter is also self-activity and does not, like sense, contain merely representations that arise when we are *affected* by things (and are thus passive), yet it can produce from its activity no other concepts than those which serve merely *to bring sensible representations under rules* and thereby to unite them in one consciousness, without which use of sensibility it would think nothing at all; but reason, on the contrary, shows in what we call "ideas" a spontaneity so pure that it thereby goes far beyond anything that sensibility can ever afford it, and proves its highest occupation in distinguishing the world of sense and the world of understanding from each other and thereby marking out limits for the understanding itself.

Because of this a rational being must regard himself *as intelligence* (hence not from the side of his lower powers) as belonging not to the world of sense but to the world of understanding; hence he has two standpoints from which he can regard himself and cognize laws for the use of his powers and consequently for all his actions; *first*, insofar as he belongs to the world of sense, under laws of nature (heteronomy); *second*, as belonging to the intelligible world, under laws which, being independent of nature, are not empirical but grounded merely in reason.

As a rational being, and thus as a being belonging to the intelligible world, the human being can never think of the causality of his own will otherwise than under the idea of freedom; for, independence from the determining causes of the world of sense (which reason must always ascribe to itself) is freedom. With the idea of freedom the concept of *autonomy* is now inseparably combined, and with the concept of autonomy the universal principle of morality, which in idea is the ground of all actions of *rational beings*, just as the law of nature is the ground of all appearances.

4:453

The suspicion that we raised above is now removed, the suspicion that a hidden circle was contained in our inference from freedom to autonomy and from the latter to the moral law – namely that we perhaps took as a ground the idea of freedom only for the sake of the moral law, so that we could afterwards infer the latter in turn from freedom, and that we were thus unable to furnish any ground at all for the moral law but could put it forward only as a *petitio principii*[e] disposed souls would gladly grant us, but never as a demonstrable[f] proposition. For we now see that when we think of ourselves as free we transfer ourselves into the world of understanding as members of it and cognize autonomy of the will along with its consequence, morality; but if we think of ourselves as put under obligation[g] we regard ourselves as belonging to the world of sense and yet at the same time to the world of understanding.

HOW IS A CATEGORICAL IMPERATIVE POSSIBLE?

A rational being counts himself, as intelligence, as belonging to the world of understanding, and only as an efficient cause belonging to this does he call his causality a *will*. On the other side he is also conscious of himself as a part of the world of sense, in which his actions are found as mere appearances of that causality; but their possibility from that causality of which we are not cognizant cannot be seen; instead, those actions as belonging to the world of sense must be regarded as determined by other appearances, namely desires and inclinations. All my actions as only a member of the world of understanding would therefore conform perfectly with the principle of autonomy of the pure will; as only a part of the world of sense they would have to be taken to conform wholly to the natural law of desires and inclinations, hence to the heteronomy of nature. (The former would rest on the supreme principle of morality, the latter on that of happiness.) But because *the world of understanding contains the ground of the world of sense and so too of its laws,* and is therefore immediately lawgiving with respect to my will (which belongs wholly to the world of understanding) and must accordingly also be thought as such, it follows that I shall cognize myself as intelligence, though on the other side as a being belonging to the world of sense, as nevertheless subject to the law of the world of understanding, that is, of reason, which contains in the idea of freedom the law of the world of understanding, and thus cognize myself as subject to the autonomy of the will; consequently the laws of the world of understanding must be regarded as imperatives for me, and actions in conformity with these as duties.

4:454

And so categorical imperatives are possible by this: that the idea of freedom makes me a member of an intelligible world and consequently, if I were only this, all my actions *would* always be in conformity with the autonomy of the will; but since at the same time I intuit myself as a member of the world of sense, they *ought* to be in conformity with it; and this *categorical* ought represents a synthetic proposition a priori, since to my will affected

[e] *Erbittung des Prinzips*
[f] *erweislichen*
[g] *als verpflichtet*

by sensible desires there is added the idea of the same will but belonging to the world of the understanding – a will pure and practical of itself, which contains the supreme condition, in accordance with reason, of the former will; this is roughly like the way in which concepts of the understanding, which by themselves signify nothing but lawful form in general, are added to intuitions of the world of sense and thereby make possible synthetic propositions a priori on which all cognition of a nature rests.

The practical use of common human reason confirms the correctness of this deduction. There is no one – not even the most hardened scoundrel, if only he is otherwise accustomed to use reason – who, when one sets before him examples of honesty of purpose, of steadfastness in following good maxims, of sympathy and general benevolence (even combined with great sacrifices of advantage and comfort), does not wish that he might also be so disposed. He cannot indeed bring this about in himself, though only because of his inclinations and impulses; yet at the same time he wishes to be free from such inclinations, which are burdensome to himself. Hence he proves, by this, that with a will free from impulses of sensibility he transfers himself in thought into an order of things altogether different from that of his desires in the field of sensibility, since from that wish he can expect no satisfaction of his desires and hence no condition[h] that would satisfy any of his actual or otherwise imaginable inclinations (for if he expected this, the very idea which elicits that wish from him would lose its preeminence); he can expect only a greater inner worth of his person. This better person, however, he believes himself to be when he transfers himself to the standpoint of a member of the world of understanding, as the idea of freedom, that is, of independence from *determining* causes of the world of sense, constrains him involuntarily[i] to do; and from this standpoint he is conscious of a good will that, by his own acknowledgments, constitutes the law for his evil will as a member of the world of sense – a law of whose authority he is cognizant even while he transgresses it. The moral "*ought*" is then his own necessary "*will*" as a member of an intelligible world, and is thought by him as "ought" only insofar as he regards himself at the same time as a member of the world of sense. 4:455

ON THE EXTREME BOUNDARY OF ALL PRACTICAL PHILOSOPHY

All human beings think of themselves as having free will.[j] From this come all judgments upon actions as being such that they *ought to have been done even though they were not done.* Yet this freedom is no concept of experi-

---

[h] *Zustand*
[i] *unwillkürlich*
[j] *denken sich dem Willen nach als frei*

ence, and moreover cannot be one, since it always remains even though experience shows the opposite of those requirements that are represented as necessary under the presupposition of freedom. On the other side, it is equally necessary that everything which takes place should be determined without exception in accordance with laws of nature; and this natural necessity is also no concept of experience, just because it brings with it the concept of necessity and hence of an a priori cognition. But this concept of a nature is confirmed by experience and must itself unavoidably be presupposed if experience, that is, coherent cognition of objects of the senses in accordance with universal laws, is to be possible. Hence freedom is only an *idea* of reason, the objective reality of which is in itself doubtful, whereas nature is a *concept of the understanding* that proves, and must necessarily prove, its reality in examples from experience.

From this there arises a dialectic of reason since, with respect to the will, the freedom ascribed to it seems to be in contradiction with natural necessity; and at this parting of the ways reason *for speculative purposes* finds the road of natural necessity much more traveled and more usable than that of freedom; yet *for practical purposes* the footpath of freedom is 4:456 the only one on which it is possible to make use of our reason in our conduct; hence it is just as impossible for the most subtle philosophy as for the most common human reason to argue freedom away. Philosophy must therefore assume that no true contradiction will be found between freedom and natural necessity in the very same human actions, for it cannot give up the concept of nature any more than that of freedom.

Nevertheless, this seeming contradiction must be removed in a convincing way, even though we shall never be able to comprehend how freedom is possible. For if even the thought of freedom contradicts itself or contradicts nature, which is equally necessary, it would have to be given up altogether in favor of natural necessity.

It would, however, be impossible to escape this contradiction if the subject who seems to himself free thought of himself *in the same sense* or *in the very same relation* when he calls himself free as when he takes himself to be subject to the law of nature with regard to the same action. Hence it is an indispensable task of speculative philosophy at least to show that its illusion[k] about the contradiction rests on our thinking of the human being in a different sense and relation when we call him free and when we hold him, as a part of nature, to be subject to its laws, and to show that both not only *can* very well coexist but also must be thought as *necessarily united* in the same subject; for otherwise no ground could be given why we should burden reason with an idea which, though it may *without contradiction* be united with another that is sufficiently established, yet entangles us in a business that brings reason into difficult straits in its theoretical use. This

[k] *Täuschung*

duty, however, is incumbent upon speculative philosophy only so that it may clear the way for practical philosophy. Hence it is not left to the philosopher's discretion whether he wants to remove the seeming conflict or leave it untouched; for, in the latter case the theory about this would be *bonum vacans,*[1] into possession of which the fatalist could justifiably enter and chase all morals from its supposed property, as occupying it without title.

Nevertheless it cannot yet be said here that the boundary of practical philosophy begins. For, the settlement of that controversy does not belong to it; instead it only requires of speculative reason that it put an end to the discord in which it entangles itself in theoretical questions, so that practical reason may have tranquillity and security from the external attacks that could make the land on which it wants to build a matter of dispute.

4:457

But the rightful claim[m] to freedom of will made even by common human reason is based on the consciousness and the granted presupposition of the independence of reason from merely subjectively determining causes, all of which together constitute what belongs only to feeling[n] and hence come under the general name of sensibility. The human being, who this way regards himself as an intelligence, thereby puts himself in a different order of things and in a relation to determining grounds of an altogether different kind when he thinks of himself as an intelligence endowed with a will, and consequently with causality, than when he perceives himself as a phenomenon in the world of sense (as he also really is) and subjects his causality to external determination in accordance with laws of nature. Now he soon becomes aware that both can take place at the same time, and indeed must do so. For, that a *thing in appearance* (belonging to the world of sense) is subject to certain laws from which *as a thing* or a being *in itself* it is independent contains not the least contradiction; that he must represent and think of himself in this twofold way, however, rests as regards the first on consciousness of himself as an object affected through the senses and as regards the second on consciousness of himself as an intelligence, that is, as independent of sensible impressions in the use of reason (hence as belonging to the world of understanding).

So it is that the human being claims for himself a will which lets nothing be put to his account that belongs merely to his desires and inclinations, and on the contrary thinks as possible by means of it – indeed as necessary – actions that can be done only by disregarding all desires and sensible incitements. The causality of such actions lies in him as intelligence and in the laws of effects and actions in accordance with principles of an intelligible world, of which he knows nothing more than

[1] i.e., something that belongs to no one
[m] *Rechtsanspruch*
[n] *Empfindung*

61

that in it reason alone, and indeed pure reason independent of sensibility, gives the law, and, in addition, that since it is there, as intelligence only, that he is his proper self (as a human being he is only the appearance of himself), those laws apply to him immediately and categorically, so that what inclinations and impulses (hence the whole nature of the world of 4:458 sense) incite him to cannot infringe upon the laws of his volition as intelligence; indeed, he does not hold himself accountable for the former or ascribe them to his proper self, that is, to his will, though he does ascribe to it the indulgence he would show them if he allowed them to influence his maxims to the detriment of the rational laws of his will.

By *thinking* itself into a world of understanding practical reason does not at all overstep its boundaries, but it would certainly do so if it wanted to *intuit* or *feel itself* into it.[o] That is only a negative thought with respect to the world of sense: it gives reason no laws for determining the will and is positive only in this single point: that freedom as a negative determination is combined with a (positive) capacity as well, and indeed with a causality of reason that we call a will, a capacity so to act that the principle of actions conforms with the essential constitution of a rational cause, that is, with the condition of universal validity of a maxim as a law. But if practical reason were to fetch in addition an *object of the will*, that is, a motive, from the world of understanding, then it would overstep its bounds and pretend to be cognizant of something of which it knows nothing. The concept of a world of understanding is thus only a *standpoint* that reason sees itself constrained to take outside appearances *in order to think of itself as practical*, as would not be possible if the influences of sensibility were determining for the human being but is nevertheless necessary insofar as he is not to be denied consciousness of himself as an intelligence and consequently as a rational cause active by means of reason, that is, operating freely.[p] This thought admittedly brings with it the idea of another order and another lawgiving than that of the mechanism of nature, which has to do with the sensible world; and it makes necessary the concept of an intelligible world (i.e., the whole of rational beings as things in themselves), but without the least pretense to think of it further than in terms merely of its *formal* condition, that is, of the universality of maxims of the will as law and so of the autonomy of the will, which alone is compatible with its freedom; on the contrary, all laws that are determined with reference to an object give heteronomy, which can be found only in laws of nature and also can have to do only with the world of sense.

But reason would overstep all its bounds if it took it upon itself to 4:459 *explain how* pure reason can be practical, which would be exactly the same task as to explain *how freedom is possible*.

---

[o] *hineinschauen, hineinempfinden*
[p] *als vernünftige und durch Vernunft tätige, d.i. frei wirkende*

For we can explain nothing but what we can reduce to laws the object of which can be given in some possible experience. Freedom, however, is a mere idea, the objective reality of which can in no way be presented in accordance with laws of nature and so too cannot be presented in any possible experience; and because no example of anything analogous^q can ever be put under it, it can never be comprehended or even only seen.^{r} It holds only as a necessary presupposition of reason in a being that believes itself to be conscious of a will, that is, of a faculty distinct from a mere faculty of desire (namely, a faculty of determining itself to action as an intelligence and hence in accordance with laws of reason independently of natural instincts). Now, where determination by laws of nature ceases, there all *explanation* ceases as well, and nothing is left but *defense*, that is, to repel the objections of those who pretend to have seen deeper into the essence of things and therefore boldly declare that freedom is impossible. We can only point out to them that the supposed contradiction they have discovered in it lies nowhere else than in this: in order to make the law of nature hold with respect to human actions they must necessarily regard the human being as an appearance; and now when they are required to think of him, as an intelligence, as also a thing in itself they nevertheless continue to regard him as appearance here too; in that case the separation^s of his causality (i.e., of his will) from all the natural laws of the world of sense in one and the same subject would be a contradiction; but this would come to nothing if they were willing to reflect and to acknowledge, as is equitable, that things in themselves (though hidden) must lie behind appearances as their ground and that one cannot insist that the laws of their operation^t should be the same as those under which their appearances stand.

The subjective impossibility of *explaining* the freedom of the will is the same as the impossibility of discovering and making comprehensible^u an *interest* which the human being can take in moral laws;* and yet he does

4:460

---

*An interest is that by which reason becomes practical, i.e., becomes a cause determining the will. Hence only of a rational being does one say that he takes an interest in something; nonrational creatures feel only sensible impulses. Reason takes an immediate interest in an action only when the universal validity of the maxim of the action is a sufficient determining ground of the will. Only such an interest is pure. But if it can determine the will only by means of another object of desire^v or on the presupposition of a special feeling of the subject, then reason takes only a mediate interest in the action, and since reason all by itself, without experience, can discover neither objects of the will nor a special feeling lying at its basis, this latter interest would be only empirical and not a pure rational interest. The logical interest of reason (to further its insights) is never immediate but presupposes purposes for its use.

^{q} *niemals nach irgend einer Analogie*
^{r} *niemals begriffen, oder auch nur eingesehen werden kann*
^{s} *Absonderung*
^{t} *Wirkungsgesetzen*
^{u} *ausfindig und begreiflich zu machen*
^{v} *des Begehrens*

really take an interest in them, the foundation of which in us we call moral feeling, which some have falsely given out as the standard for our moral appraisal whereas it must rather be regarded as the *subjective* effect that the law exercises on the will, to which reason alone delivers the objective grounds.

In order for a sensibly affected rational being to will that for which reason alone prescribes the "ought," it is admittedly required that his reason have the capacity to *induce a feeling of pleasure* or of delight in the fulfillment of duty, and thus there is required a causality of reason to determine sensibility in conformity with its principles. But it is quite impossible to see, that is, to make comprehensible a priori,^{w} how a mere thought which itself contains nothing sensible produces a feeling^x of pleasure or displeasure; for that is a special kind of causality about which, as about any causality, we can determine nothing whatever a priori but must for this consult experience alone. But since this cannot provide us with any relation of cause to effect except between two objects of experience – whereas here pure reason, by means of mere ideas (which yield no object at all for experience), is to be the cause of an effect that admittedly lies in experience – it follows that for us human beings it is quite impossible to explain how and why the *universality of a maxim as law* and hence morality interests us. This much only is certain: it is not *because the law interests* us that it has validity for us (for that is heteronomy and dependence of

4:461 practical reason upon sensibility, namely upon a feeling lying at its basis, in which case it could never be morally lawgiving); instead, the law interests because it is valid for us as human beings, since it arose from our will as intelligence and so from our proper self; *but what belongs to mere appearance is necessarily subordinated by reason to the constitution of the thing in itself.*

Thus the question, how a categorical imperative is possible, can indeed be answered to the extent that one can furnish the sole presupposition on which alone it is possible, namely the idea of freedom, and that one can also see the necessity of this presupposition, which is sufficient for the *practical use* of reason, that is, for the conviction of the *validity of this imperative* and so also of the moral law; but how this presupposition itself is possible can never be seen by any human reason. On the presupposition of the freedom of the will of an intelligence, however, its *autonomy,* as the formal condition under which alone it can be determined, is a necessary consequence. Moreover, to presuppose this freedom of the will is (as speculative philosophy can show) not only quite *possible* (without falling into contradiction with the principle of natural necessity in the connection of appearances in the world of sense); it is also practically *necessary* – that is, necessary in idea, without any further condition – for a rational being

---

^{w} *einzusehen, d.i. a priori begreiflich zu machen*
^{x} *Empfindung*

who is conscious of his causality through reason and so of a will (which is distinct from desires) to put it under all his voluntary[y] actions as their condition. But it is quite beyond the capacity of any human reason to explain *how* pure reason, without other incentives that might be taken from elsewhere, can be of itself practical, that is, how the mere *principle of the universal validity of all its maxims as laws* (which would admittedly be the form of a pure practical reason), without any matter (object) of the will in which one could take some interest in advance, can of itself furnish an incentive and produce an interest that would be called purely *moral;* it is impossible for us to explain, in other words, *how pure reason can be practical,* and all the pains and labor of seeking an explanation of it are lost.

It is just the same as if I tried to fathom how freedom itself as the causality of a will is possible. For then I leave the philosophic ground of explanation behind and I have no other. I might indeed revel[z] in the intelligible world, the world of intelligences, which is still left to me; but even though I have an *idea* of it, which has its good grounds, yet I have not the least *cognizance* of it nor can I ever attain this by all the efforts of my natural faculty of reason. It signifies only a "something" that is left over when I have excluded from the determining grounds of my will everything belonging to the world of sense, merely in order to limit the principle of motives from the field of sensibility by circumscribing this field and showing that it does not include everything within itself[a] but that there is still more beyond it; but of this something more I have no further cognizance. As for pure reason, which thinks this ideal: after its isolation from all matter, that is, cognition of objects, nothing is left for me but the form of it – namely the practical law of the universal validity of maxims – and to think of reason, conformably with this, with reference to a pure world of understanding as a possible efficient cause, that is, a cause determining the will. Here an incentive must be quite lacking; for this idea of an intelligible world would itself have to be the incentive or that in which reason originally takes an interest; but to make this comprehensible is precisely the problem that we cannot solve.

4:462

Here, then, is the highest[b] limit of all moral inquiry; and it is already of great importance to determine it just so that reason may not, on the one hand, to the detriment of morals search about in the world of sense for the supreme motive and a comprehensible but empirical interest, and that it may not, on the other hand, impotently flap its wings without moving from the spot in the space, which is empty for it, of transcendent concepts

---

[y] *willkürlichen*
[z] *herumschwärmen*
[a] *Alles in Allem in sich fasse*
[b] *oberste.* Given the heading of the division beginning on 455, one would have expected *äußerste,* "extreme."

65

called the intelligible world, and so lose itself among phantoms. Moreover, the idea of a pure world of understanding as a whole of all intelligences, to which we ourselves belong as rational beings (though on the other side we are also members of the world of sense), remains always a useful and permitted idea for the sake of a rational belief, even if all knowledge stops at its boundary – useful and permitted for producing in us a lively interest in the moral law by means of the noble ideal of a universal kingdom of *ends in themselves* (rational beings) to which we can

4:463 belong as members only when we carefully conduct ourselves in accordance with maxims of freedom as if they were laws of nature.

CONCLUDING REMARK

The speculative use of reason *with respect to nature* leads to the absolute necessity of some supreme cause of the *world:* the practical use of reason *with regard to freedom* leads also to an absolute necessity, but only *of laws of actions* of a rational being as such. Now, it is an essential *principle* of every use of our reason to push its cognition to consciousness of its *necessity* (for without this it would not be cognition on the part of reason). It is, however, an equally essential *limitation* of this same reason that it can see neither the *necessity* of what is and what happens nor the necessity of what ought to happen unless a *condition* under which it is and happens or ought to happen is put at the basis of this. In this way, however, by constant inquiry after the condition, the satisfaction of reason is only further and further postponed. Hence it restlessly seeks the unconditionally necessary and sees itself constrained to assume it without any means of making it comprehensible to itself, fortunate enough if it can discover only the concept that is compatible with this presupposition. It is therefore no censure of our deduction of the supreme principle of morality, but a reproach that must be brought against human reason in general, that it cannot make comprehensible as regards its absolute necessity an unconditional practical law (such as the categorical imperative must be); for, that it is unwilling to do this through a condition – namely by means of some interest laid down as a basis – cannot be held against it, since then it would not be the moral law, that is, the supreme law of freedom. And thus we do not indeed comprehend the practical unconditional necessity of the moral imperative, but we nevertheless comprehend its *incomprehensibility;* and this is all that can fairly be required of a philosophy that strives in its principles to the very boundary of human reason.

Notes

1 Christian Wolff's *Philosophia Practica Universalis* was published in two volumes in 1738–9. Kant himself uses *"Philosophia practica universalis"* as the subtitle of Section III of his Introduction to *The Metaphysics of Morals* (6:221–8), the title of which is "Concepts Preliminary to the Metaphysics of Morals" and in which he discusses concepts common to both *The Doctrine of Right* and *The Doctrine of Virtue*.

2 Kant did plan to publish a work having this title; he apparently did not, however, intend to write a work entitled *Critique of Practical Reason*. I take it that he is here referring to subject matter rather than titles, and I have therefore capitalized neither. However, since a sharp distinction should be drawn between the proposed book that he calls "a metaphysics of morals" and the "metaphysics of morals" to which Section II of the *Groundwork* makes the "transition," I have marked the distinction by retaining his definite or indefinite article in the case of the former while omitting it in the case of the latter.

3 On the sense of *Verstand*, *Witz*, and *Urteilskraft* that is relevant in this context, see *Anthropology from a Pragmatic Point of View* (7:196–201). On "character" in the general sense in which the word is used in this sentence, see ibid., 7:249, 291–6.

4 Johann Georg Sulzer (1720–79), who in 1775 became director of the philosophic division of the Berlin Academy. He was best known for his writings in aesthetics, especially his *Allgemeine Theorie der Schönen Künste*.

5 *Weltklugheit*, or prudence regarding the world. Compare pragmatic *Weltkenntniss* in 7:120; also 271 ff.

6 In his *Inquiry into the Original of Our Ideas of Beauty and Virtue* (1725) and *Essay on the Nature and Conduct of the Passions and Affections and Illustrations upon the Moral Sense* (1728), Francis Hutcheson maintained that we make moral distinctions and are motivated to virtuous actions not through reason but through a moral sense, by means of which benevolence pleases us.

Selected glossary

act	Akt
action	Handlung
activity	Tätigkeit
agreeable	angenehm
appearance	Erscheinung
approve	billigen
beneficence	Wohltätigkeit, Wohltun
benevolence	Wohlwollen
bind	verbinden
bound(ary)	Grenze
capacity	Vermögen
cause	Ursache
choice (power of)	Willkür
choose	wählen
coercion	Zwang
cognition	Erkenntnis
cognize	erkennen
concept	Begriff
condition	Bedingung, Zustand
consent	Einwilligung
consequence	Folgerung
constraint	Nötigung, Zwang
contempt	Verachtung
desire	Begierde
determination	Bestimmung
determine	bestimmen
dignity	Würde
disapprove	mißbilligen
displeasure	Unlust
disposition	Gesinnung
duty	Pflicht
effect	Wirkung
employment	Gebrauch
end	Zweck

enjoyment	Genuß
evil	Böse
example	Beispiel
experience	Erahrung
explanation	Erklärung
explicate	entwickeln
faith	Glaube
feeling	Gefühl, Empfindung
final end	Endzweck
final purpose	Endabsicht
general	allgemein
happiness	Glückseligkeit
holiness	Heiligkeit
honest	ehrlich
honor	Ehre
human	menschlich
human being	Mensch
humanity	Menschheit, Menschlichkeit, Humanität
impulse	Trieb, Antrieb
impurity	Unlauterkeit
incentive	Triebfeder
inclination	Neigung
innocence	Unschuld
insight	Einsicht
intention	Absicht, Vorsatz
intuition	Anschauung (*intuitus*)
judgment	Urteil, Urteilskraft
kingdom	Reich
know	wissen, kennen
knowledge	Wissen, Kenntnis
lawfulness	Gesetzmäßigkeit
lawgiver	Gesetzgeber
legislation	Gesetzgebung
legislator	Gesetzgeber
morality, morals	Sitten, Sittlichkeit, Moral, Moralität
motive	Bewegungsgrund, Bestimmungsgrund
necessitate	nötigen
necessity	Notwendigkeit
need	Bedürfnis

obligation	Verpflichtung, Verbindung
omission	Unterlassung
perfect	vollkommen
perfection	Vollkommenheit
permission	Erlaubnis
philanthropy	Menschenliebe
please	gefallen (v.r.)
pleasure	Lust
principle	Grundsatz, Prinzip
propensity	Hang
prudence	Klugheit
purpose	Absicht
purposiveness	Zweckmäßigkeit
reason	Vernunft
receptivity	Empfänglichkeit
representation	Vorstellung
resistance	Widerstand
respect	Achtung
right (n.)	Recht
rightful	rechtlich
self-conceit	Eigendünkel
self-love	Eigenliebe, Selbstliebe
sensation	Empfindung
sense(s)	Sinn(e)
sensibility	Sinnlichkeit
spontaneity	Selbsttätigkeit
sublime	erhaben
supreme	oberst
sympathy	Teilnehmung
understanding	Verstand
universal	allgemein
universal validity	Allgemeingültigkeit
use	Gebrauch
validity	Gültigkeit
vice	Laster
virtue	Tugend
volition	Wollen
voluntary	willkürlich, freiwillig
will	Wille
worth	Wert
worthiness	Würdigkeit
wrong	unrecht (tun)

Index

a priori vs. a posteriori, viii–ix, 5
analytic vs. synthetic judgments, viii–ix, xxiv;
   imperatives of skill are analytic, 28;
   imperatives of prudence would be
   analytic if happiness were a determinate
   concept, 28–9; but imperatives of
   morality are synthetic, 30, 47, 51, 53;
   difficulties of establishing synthetic
   principles, 29–30, 51; how to establish
   synthetic propositions, 53
analytic vs. synthetic methods of
   presentation, xi, xvi, xxiv, 5–6
anthropology, practical, 2, 3, 22, 23
appearance and reality, xxvi–xxvii, 56; we
   cannot cognize what we are in ourselves
   through inner sensation, 56; insofar as
   we are receptive we belong to the world
   of sense, but insofar as we are active we
   belong to the intellectual world, 56, 61;
   common understanding wants to make
   reality or things in themselves objects of
   intuition, 57; things in themselves must
   lie behind appearances, 63; see also
   intelligible world; two standpoints
autonomy, 41; appropriate motivation for a
   categorical imperative, xxii–xxiii, 40–1;
   failure to grasp this is the reason why all
   previous moral philosophy has failed,
   40–1; and free will, xxiv–xxv, 52, 55,
   57–8, 64; if we belonged wholly to the
   world of understanding, actions would
   conform perfectly to the law of
   autonomy, 58, 62; see also autonomy,
   formula of; heteronomy
autonomy, formula of: argument for, 39–41;
   stated, 47; formula of autonomy in the
   kingdom of ends corresponds to the
   complete determination of all maxims,
   44; can be arrived at by analyzing the
   concept of morality, 47; but is a
   synthetic principle, 47

beneficence, duty of, as derived from the
   Formula of Universal Law, 33; as
   derived from the Formula of the
   Humanity, 39
beneficence, good-willed vs. naturally
   sympathetic, xii–xiv, 11–12

categorical imperative: its content or
   principle may be derived from its
   concept, xvi–xvii, 30–1; as a synthetic
   principle, xvi, 47, 58–9; duty must be
   expressed in categorical imperatives, 34;
   categorical imperatives and autonomous
   motivation, xxii–xxiii, 40–1, 47–50;
   relation between the three formulas of,
   43–4; as the law of the free will, 52–3;
   see also autonomy, formula of; humanity,
   formula of; kingdom of ends; moral law;
   morality, imperatives of; universal law,
   formula of
causality, of the will, 52; and the two
   standpoints, 56, 58; see also autonomy
cause, principle that every event has a cause,
   ix–x, ix n.3, xxvi
character, 7, 12
circle, appears in the argument for the moral
   law, xxvi, 55–6; argument not circular
   after all, 57–8
coercion, xxi
contradictions, interpretations of,
   xviii–xix
contradictions in conception vs.
   contradictions in the will, xix
Copernican Revolution, in Kant's philosophy
   in general, vii; in ethics, xxiii
critique of pure practical reason, 5

deception, xxi
determinism, xxvi–xxvii; apparent conflict
   between freedom and determinism gives
   rise to a dialectic of reason, 60; this
   resolved by appeal to the two
   standpoints, 60–2; only what falls
   under natural determinism can be
   explained, 63
dignity, 42–3; morality as the ground of
   dignity, 42; autonomy as the ground of
   dignity, 43, 45, 46
divine will, not the basis of morality, xvi–xvii,
   49; see also God
duties, categories or divisions of, 31n, 33;
   see also duties to oneself and duties to
   others; perfect and imperfect duties;
   strict and wide duties
duties to oneself and duties to others, 31

71

duty, 2, 4; defined, 10, 46; action from, xii; distinguished from actions done from self-interest, 10–11; distinguished from actions done from immediate inclination, 11–13; moral worth of actions from duty depends on the agent's principle of volition rather than his purpose, 13, 14; defined as the necessity of an action from respect for law, 13, 14, 16; formula of universal law as the principle of, 15–16

empiricism, viii
ends, role in volition, xx, 36; objective vs. subjective, 36, 37; relative ends vs. ends in themselves, 36, 37; rational nature is an end-in-itself, 37; rational nature sets ends, 44; *see also* ends in itself
ends in itself, viii, xxi, 36ff.; we are ends in ourselves in virtue of lawgiving, 42; morality makes us ends in ourselves, 42; autonomy makes us ends in ourselves, 43; ends in themselves are conceived as existing things not to act against rather than ends to be effected, 44–5; end in itself must be the subject of all ends, 45; *see also* ends, role in volition
ethics, philosophical treatment of, 1–5; need for an *a priori* part, 2–4
examples, relevance to moral philosophy, xv, 19–20
exceptions, we make exceptions of ourselves when we violate duties, 33–4

false promise, example of, 15; under the formula of universal law, xvii–xviii, 32; under the formula of humanity, xxi–xxii, 38
forbidden, xix; means the action does not accord with autonomy, 46
formal vs. material, x, xiv n.7, 1; the will must be determined by the formal principle of volition, 13; defined, 36
formula of autonomy, *see* autonomy, formula of
formula of humanity, *see* humanity, formula of
formula of universal law, *see* universal law, formula of
formula of universal law of nature, *see* universal law, formula of
freedom: as independence of determination by alien causes, xxiv, 52; positive and negative, xxiv, 52–3, 62; why the will's freedom must be autonomy, 52–3; a free will is a will under moral laws, 53; morality follows analytically from freedom, 53; points us to the conception

of the intelligible world, 53, 62; must be presupposed as a property of rational wills, 53–4; rational beings must act under the idea of freedom, xxv, 53–4; presupposition of freedom leads to consciousness of moral law, 54; idea of freedom seems to presuppose autonomy and morality, 55; connection between freedom and morality seems to make the argument for morality circular, 55–8; since freedom and autonomy are reciprocal concepts, 55; but argument is not circular, 57–8; when we think of ourselves as free we think of ourselves as members of the world of understanding, 58, 59, 62; all human beings think of themselves as having free will and so as being obligated, 59; freedom not a concept of experience, 59–60; dialectic of reason arising from the apparent conflict of freedom and determinism resolved by appeal to the two standpoints, xxvi–xxvii, 60–2; objective reality of, cannot be proved, 60, 63; we cannot explain how it is possible, 62–5; *see also* autonomy
friendship, 20

God, as morally perfect, 21; as the sovereign of the kingdom of ends, 41; as a sovereign under whom the kingdom of ends and the kingdom of nature may be united, 46; good will, 7–10; as a condition of the value of happiness, 7, 10; as a condition of the value of talents and personal qualities, 7–8, 42; as a condition of value in general, xi, 10; value rests in the nature of its volition itself, xii, 8; is good in itself, 8, 10; value is independent of usefulness or fruitfulness, 8; value is independent of its purposes, 13, 14; is the natural purpose of the rational will, 8–10; explication of the good will to find its principle, 10–16; is motivated by the representation of law itself, 14–15; must be autonomous, 50; why the good will's principle must be that of acting on maxims which can be universal law, 14–16; its formula is the categorical imperative, 44, 53; even the most hardened scoundrel is conscious of a good will that constitutes a law for him, 59

happiness, value conditioned by the good will, xi, 7, 10; not the natural purpose of the rational will, 8–10, 14; not the basis

Cambridge texts in the history of philosophy

Titles published in the series thus far